CW01084648

36" or Bust!
A Pennine Way
Challenge

D.J. Smithers

Copyright © 2012
D.J.Smithers

All rights reserved. No part of this book may be
reproduced in any form, except for the inclusion of brief
quotations in reviews, without the written permission of
the author.

www.davidjohn37.co.uk

I would like to thank my ex-wife, Sandy, (we divorced two years after this book was written but have stayed the best of friends) for all the support she gave me with my endeavours throughout our marriage, and to my two beautiful children, Jamie & Kris, who likewise have always humoured Dad's flights of fancy. Also, big thanks to Sam for trying to inject some the level-headedness into my life and helping me keep somewhat grounded. Well, he tried anyway.

Preface

First of all, I want it known that I'm totally blameless for all this tomfoolery, this hair-brain of an idea that an overweight, out of condition, weekend camper could conquer a gruelling, bog-infested, ankle-twisting, 270 miles along England's back-breaking backbone they call the Pennine Way. No, that onus lies totally in the lap of four other gentlemen, namely; Wainwright, Stephenson, Noakes and Pilton. A couple of them you may be familiar but one or two names may elude you, so let me clarify.

Firstly, the late and sadly missed, Alfred Wainwright. That grand old gentleman of the walking fraternity whose immaculate and beautifully hand-drawn and hand-written books on the Lakeland fells and Pennine Way amongst others, have become the backpackers 'Bible', and who sadly passed away in 1991 leaving a void that will never be filled.

Secondly, Tom Stephenson; originator of the Way back in 1965 and without who's tenacity it may never have been possible to gain access to most of the countryside along the route.

Then there's John Noakes, one-time presenter of Blue Peter back in the early 70's who went on to host his own series of programmes entitled 'Go with Noakes'. One of the episodes was an attempt on the Way which was probably the first ever showing of the long distance walk on T.V. and which whetted my appetite and planted the seeds of adventure in me.

Lastly, there's Barry Pilton. Not a name that immediately rings any bells at the mention but as far as my endeavours are concerned somebody who played an important part. A television presenter? No. A writer of authoritative books perhaps? Not as such. An intrepid explorer then? Not likely! No, Mr. B. Pilton was just a simple, amateur backpacker like me who challenged the Pennine Way and won by the skin of his teeth and put to paper all that happened both serious and funny in a tome entitled One Man and his Bog, and it was this that made me more than ever to try it myself just to find out if there could be anything funny on the toughest, longest, continuous walk in Britain.

The following pages are my account of what happened when I attempted the Way (twice) and finally won. Of how I started out overweight and unfit and finished a hell of a lot lighter. Of how I set out a man and ended up still a man, just further away. Of the endless struggle between me and....well, me really! I write it as it happened and how it happened and tell it like it is – honest!

36" or Bust!
A Pennine Way
Challenge.

Chapter 1
Early Days

My first real taste of camping was back in my early teens when, at the tender but impressionable age of 13, I became a Royal Marine cadet with a vain hope that within a couple of years I'd be the SAS's youngest ever recruit, seeing in me a fearless warrior who, once I'd cured myself of timidness, acne, two left feet, cack-handedness and a pigeon chest, would welcome me with open arms to their elite band of brothers. Alas, the constant verbal abuse and thumping's I got from the other cadets put paid my military career within a year, plus I didn't like the way my C.O. shouted at me! The first night's training really should have forewarned me of what was to come. I was approached by a cadet some three years older than me; he held out his hand to shake mine, then promptly kneed me in the nuts! Being young and naive I just assumed that this was how tough army men greeted each other, but then it only seemed to happen to me, constantly? During that year we did get to go on a couple of exercises. One of which consisted of three of us cadets huddled together for warmth in a draughty tent that had no sewn-in groundsheet, camped around a lake for two nights. And, to make it more soldierly, we had to take turns at night sentry duty. I can still remember my stint at 2 am standing in a sentry box, young, alone and scared witless, looking out onto a mist-enshrouded lake with the sound of a thousand wild creatures around me. I remember thinking 'If this is camping, you can stuff it!'

It wasn't until three years later that my next encounter under canvas reared its ugly head.

It was an invitation by my local youth club to help represent them in an inter-club competition. It wasn't too far removed from my first effort in that the tents used were the old Scout type with no sewn in groundsheet and tie-up flaps. I can't remember much about the weekend accept that on the Sunday we were due to float a hand-built raft on the lake. This was crafted out of wooden pallets with large plastic bottles strapped to the sides for buoyancy and a piece of rough 4"x2" timber handrail going from one side to the other. On the Saturday night, while all the others were enjoying a disco in the marquee, I, being a bit of a loner, decided to whittle the said 4"x2" into a smooth, rounded, splinterless handrail. This took a good 2 to 3 hours as I only had a small, blunt knife, but I was determined. By mornings early light everybody was totally impressed by my efforts from the night before and I received many a pat on the back and word of thanks from the 'crew'. Feeling pretty chuffed at my work and the recognition I received I helped lift her to the water's edge and felt proud as I looked around to see that none of the other 'rafters' had offered the same meticulous care to their efforts that I had, and that surely my labours must add points to our team score? We proudly loaded the raft onto the slipway, stood back in admiration and watch her slide gracefully into the water. We then all watched open mouthed as it slowly, but still gracefully, turned turtle. I felt my proud demeanour crumble into despair. All those hours of work! All those cuts and blisters! All that sweat and toil! All for nothing! The only ones admiring my beautifully crafted handrail now were a few frogs and the odd newt. I cried.

A year later I was invited back again, but this time to help out on a Duke of Edinburgh award weekend. I, along with a friend, was given the task of teaching young hopefuls the finer points of map and compass reading, which I thought I knew extensively due to my 'military background', and he thought he knew due to him being a Boy Scout once. After 30 minutes and countless arguments which nearly ended up with the two of us coming to blows over how to perform this simple task, the DoE's, having looked on in total bewilderment, eventually wandered off and got lost without our help. Alas, I was never invited again.

Cumbria became the place of camping proper and started my lifelong love of both the Lake District and backpacking.

The year was 1974 and six of us, three girls and three boys, decided to have one of those holidays that all teenagers dream of. One without their parents. Even though we were all around the 17/18 mark it took some persuading of the girl's dads to let them go. Eventually, they gave in after we convinced them that we were taking two large frame tents, one for the boys and one for the girls. Yeah, right! Two tents we did take but the arrangement was that each couple had two nights alone in one of the tents to do as they wished, be it Monopoly, Scrabble, naked I-Spy!

It was obvious right from the start that all of us lacked any camping sense. This was made plain when we turned up at Victoria coach station in London loaded down with suitcases, holdalls, rucksacks, two large tents and enough camping equipment to supplement a large Scout troop. When we finally arrived at Penrith we had to hire two taxis just to take all our luggage and equipment to the campsite, then come back for us! It turned out to be one of the best holidays ever spent under canvas and one which we tried to repeat two years later without success. Practically every year after that has been spent on a camping holiday, much to the annoyance of my family. For some reason, my children preferred the seaside, and so every year we would have the same arguments.

"But kids," I would say, "Camping's healthier for you."

And back would come the reply, "But we prefer the seaside!"

"Yes I know," I would protest, "But just think of all the fresh air of the countryside?"
"But we like the seaside!"
I'd try again. "But imagine all the dirt and filth in the water and the polluted beaches and the crowded arcades and the noise?"
"But we want to go to the seaside!"

So, in the end, we came to a compromise. We would spend one-week camping in The Lakes or Yorkshire or Derbyshire etc, then I would show them pictures of Southend. I was a cruel father.

In the years preceding my eventual conquest of the Pennine Way I had approached three different friends in the hope of gaining a walking partner, all three attempts ended in failure. The first was Gary, an old school friend. All was going well until he started questioning the mileage needed to be walked each day. When I pointed out that some days we would have to cover 25mls and not all of it flat, that was enough to cast doubts on his commitment, and so he passed up the invitation. Next was Sam, up for the challenge, didn't mind the slog but would only do it if his wife could come as well and, as she wasn't interested, another friend bit the dust. The last of the hopefuls was Mick, my next-door neighbour who was a fireman and Scout leader. He was fit, used to the outdoor life, often went backpacking and had a wife who didn't mind him going off without her. Perfect! This was the closest yet. We planned the walk meticulously, bought all the necessary equipment, booked the appropriate time off work and counted down the days to the walk. Unfortunately, six weeks before the walk he went and badly sprained his ankle on a call-out! As the two weeks were already booked off and, as Mick felt really guilty about letting me down, we instead settled for some low-level walking, or hobbling in his case, in the Lake District.

What should have lasted a fortnight ended after just four days with both of us being stuck inside the tent due to constant bad weather, an eventual broken ridge pole and empty pockets. We called it a day and came home to the inevitable derision from the spouses. But I learnt a lot about lightweight camping. It was after this last effort I came to the realization that if I wanted to achieve such an ambition, then I would probably have to do it on my own.

Chapter 2
Preparation

On May of '85, I decided that if I was going to attempt something as demanding as the Pennine Way, then I'd better get some proper training behind me. So I enrolled on a weekend hill survival course in the Lake District. I decided on attending in May reasoning that I should just miss the last of the winter's snows and pre-empt the first of the summer burns. Unfortunately, it turned out to be one of the best weekends they'd had all year with bright warm days and clear, cloudless, moonlit nights, making the night time navigation exercise a complete doddle! So good was the weather in fact that it prompted the more miserly among us, well me anyway, to ask for my money back as surviving in glorious weather is something I was already proficient at, but to no avail.

When I announced in 1988 that I was finally to make an attempt on the Way the following year it was met with some scepticism on the part of my wife and a lot of derision on the part of my workmates. One, in particular, Steve, a young 'mate' we had working with us on a building site, remarked that I would probably last one mile for every inch of my gut, around 36"! (Now you see the reason for the strange title of this book.) The last laugh was on him though because my first attempt ended after only 31 miles! There were two main reasons for this.

Firstly, I had gained small blisters between the balls of my feet and my toes, which, due to their close proximity, proved to be painful although not really enough to force me to give up. It was the second reason that counted more towards my defeat, and it was purely psychological. So many people had told me that I wouldn't last, that I was too old (I was only 36?), that it was too tough, that it was a stupid thing to do, that in the end, I convinced myself they were right. And so, only three days in, I duly gave up and went home.

But, dear reader, I can now reveal here for the first time something that up until now I had kept from the world. Something that is so humiliating that only now I am willing to admit to. It's not something I'm proud of but it happened and I'll have to live with the shame. I can now own up to the REAL reason for abandoning the Pennine Way. I forgot to take my bloody cagoule! Every walker, be it man, woman or child, be it a hardy days slog or a gentle afternoon amble, would never be caught dead without their trusty cagoule. Even on a boiling hot summer's day, you take one 'Just in case!' It is to the walker what the notebook is to the novelist, or the calculator to the accountant, or the lawyer to the MP: you never go anywhere without one! Yes I know it's unforgivable, I know it's the last thing no self-respecting backpacker would ever overlook, but I did. I'm not proud of myself and I know it's something I'll have to live with for the rest of my life, but with medical help, I'm sure I'll come to terms with it.

To a certain degree, the first attempt was a disaster from the off, and not just because of the premature ending. There is one golden rule when navigating: ALWAYS TRUST YOUR COMPASS! This I ignored a couple of times to my detriment. The first was on Black Hill where, after reaching the trig point, I took a compass bearing which showed a direction of travel to the NW, but standing proud in front of me was a row of marker stakes disappearing in a north-easterly direction. So, assuming that my navigational skills were not up to scratch, I followed the posts. The path I took was known as the Wessenden Alternative and, although not the official path, it is one used by many walkers as an emergency route if the other way is too boggy, which is nearly always, and added unwanted extra miles and time to my day. The second navigational hiccup was on Northern Rotcher at Standedge where the main path looked as if it headed west but the compass indicated north. So once again I disputed my map reading skills and attempted to follow the path I thought I should be on, and once again I was proved wrong, except this time there was no alternative route. I ended up against the barbed wire fence which skirts the A640 about half a mile down from where I should have crossed it, losing an hour in so doing. When I finally reached the White House Inn I had made two bad navigational errors, was walking like a ruptured duck because of the blisters and, worse still, I had allowed the dubiousness and disparagement of those around me to defeat me. And to cap it all it started raining, hard, which is when I found out about my cagoule. So I had a couple of pints to drown my sorrows, stuffed my face with steak and kidney pie and caught the bus to Halifax to start the long journey home a broken man, vowing that I would never return. If only I could keep my promises.

Chapter 3
Late training

Day; zero – 2

Unbeknown to my employers at the time I had skipped off work early that day and had driven at breakneck speed from the building site I was working on to catch the mid-day train from Harlow to Liverpool St station where, if I kept running and used the momentum of my 50lb rucksack, I could reach St Pancras station 20 minutes before the train to Sheffield left. This was executed with such military precision that I actually reached St Pancras 45 mins before it left, leaving me to entertain myself for a good half hour before they would let anybody on the train.

As soon as we were given the all clear to board I quickly searched for somewhere that was near to the buffet car. I found a double seat and, in a totally unsociable manner, pulled the drinks tray down and placed some half-eaten sandwiches and empty coke cans on it to make it look like it was occupied already in the hope of discouraging wayward travellers with a mine of information on the horse-power, loading capacity, mechanical engineering and livery of the Midland Railway Inter-City 125 express locomotive from sitting down and imparting all their useless information to me. This done I settled down to spend the next 2 ½ hours journeying through this green and pleasant land we call England. It was pleasing to leave behind the dirt and grime and unpleasantness of suburban London with its boarded-up blocks of flats, abandoned warehouses and run down housing estates, and escape into the quietude and greenness of the surrounding rural counties. I'm afraid I have an aversion to large towns and cities. If I could afford to move to the peacefulness of a small village nestled somewhere in this green and pleasant land, I would, but until then I'm stuck in an urban sprawl in Essex.

We eventually pulled into Sheffield station at around 5 pm and already I was feeling drained as if the first minor battle of a long campaign had been fought. This was due in part to a gaggle of screaming kids running up and down the carriage with equally vocal mothers whose orders to sit down and shut up were ignored out of hand, eventually deciding that kids will be kids and letting them get on with it. This was interspersed with four half-inebriated Geordies downing innumerable pints of Newcastle Brown Ale in the buffet car and then insisting on using the toilet that was situated behind me, falling over the rampaging kids at each attempt to do so. The result was a sprawling mass of intoxicated northerners uttering unintelligible profanities at the unruly brood who, to give them their due, gave as good as they got, and irate mothers whose language needed no interpretation at all trying to extricate what was left of their kids from under the melee!

From the station to my friend Sam's house on the outskirts of Sheffield was a five-mile walk or a £6 taxi ride, so I compromised and caught a 70p bus that stopped 1½ miles down the road from his village and walked the rest. Sam & I go back a long way, back in fact to the early '70s where the hippy era was still flourishing and where we were both long-haired, velvet-jacketed, Afghan wearing drop-outs; although we both had good jobs and lived at home with our mums, which made us long-haired, velvet-jacketed, Afghan wearing conscientious drop-outs. We'd gone through a lot together, mainly music wise, where he played the guitar and I the drums and, along with a friend, formed a band called Fungus, which our mothers thought very apt. We spent many a booze-drenched evening together. The worst being when aged around 16, we downed two straight bottles of Bacardi in his bedroom while at the same time trying to play trumps. Trouble was that he had a red bulb for a light, which meant that in my eventual inebriated condition couldn't tell the difference between hearts and diamonds and kept showing him my cards so he could help me out! It was while I was in this drunken stupor that a strange thing happened? I got up to answer the call of nature and, due to the now non-existence of my legs, promptly fell over again. But when I eventually stood up again I had blood pouring out of my right hand from a deep cut, but, try as we might, we could find nothing on the floor which could have caused it? There was no ring pull, no broken glass, no sharp edges, nothing? Trouble was our intoxicated brains found this hysterically funny, regardless of the fact I could have been bleeding to death? Eventually, with my bloody handprints all over the carpet, walls and bedclothes, his mum threw me out. I was extremely ill that night, and the most of next day, and ever since have had a loathing for Bacardi, I can't even stand the smell of it without my head starting to spin.

Sam was fortunate in that he had managed to secure a good job with the civil service which eventually enabled him to move first to Sheffield, and then to a small village called Ringinglow on the edge of the South York Moors, which was ideal for him as he was a walker and runner. More fortunate was the local pub situated right next door which, knowing Sam, was probably more through choice that luck. At this precise moment in time, he needed cheering up as his mother had just died and his wife had decided to leave him. To most people, it would have been enough to send them into deep depression or even contemplate suicide, but Sam just accepted it as part of life and got on with it. I always described him as being a level-headed, down to earth; live for the moment sort of guy. He always described me as mostly being away with the fairies!

That evening we partook of some local beverages; tea, coffee, hot chocolate etc, and staggered back to his place (the tea must have been spiked?), to finish off two bottles of wine and a half pint of sherry each. The reason for the sherry was that I was extolling the virtues of a good port; unfortunately, sherry is no substitute for a good port. It was while in this relaxed-as-a-newt state that I started to pour forth all my worldly problems safe in the knowledge that my good and trusted friend was listening quietly and intently like an enlightened mentor, just waiting to offer words of solace and guidance, even at 2 am. It was the sudden loud snoring that alerted me to the reason for his quietude.

The next morning saw us both rising at 8 am, honest! Trouble was that I had a small hangover. But after eggs, bacon, tomatoes and gallons of tea, with a few hundredweight of painkillers thrown in for good measure, I managed to bring my brain back into some sought of working order. We decided to take a small hike over Burbage Rocks and Stanage Edge as a sort of pre-walk walk, stopping mid-day for a couple of glasses of lemonade. With my head still complaining about my nocturnal habits I was in no mood for more alcohol. We walked around 10 miles in all as a sort of pre-walk walk, talking about nothing in particular, except me grizzling about how nothing goes right in my life, and the wife and I not seeing eye-to-eye anymore, and having to live in a concrete jungle surrounded by dirt and decay, and having to work on building sites with people whose I.Q. is only about 2 points above that of an amoeba, and why couldn't I have married Sam Fox? Like I said; nothing in particular?

That evening we trundled off to a pub in Sheffield picking up a friend of Sam's on the way called Harry where a local American (?) band called Strongheart played very convincing copies of Led Zeppelin and Jimi Hendrix numbers. Unfortunately, I did a very convincing copy of a drunk, which is not the wisest thing to do the night before embarking on the toughest, longest, continuous footpath in Great Britain.

When we eventually arrived back at the house sometime around midnight, an unfortunate event occurred that didn't really sink in at the time but which I was going to regret when sober the next morning.

Sam's backdoor is situated some four feet above ground level and is reached by scaling some concrete steps which have no handrail or safety net, and no light. While he was trying to locate the lock I, in my half-cut state, thought it would be amusing to keep knocking the back of his knees to try to get him to collapse in a heap. Problem is that what an alcohol-filled brain perceives as being hysterically funny is actually only occurring within the grey matter of the intoxicated, whilst to the sober party, or recipient, is extremely bloody annoying, which it would be when you been unable to have a drink all night because you were driving and everybody else is 'smashed out of us brains!' as they say up north. The result being that his elbow, in a purely reflex action, obviously, made contact with my ribs sending me in a backwards direction. This is where my years of martial arts training came into their own. Sensing the possibility of a fall into the abyss I decided to leap gazelle-like and land on the bottom step. Unfortunately I landed totally un-gazelle like in a heap on the ground where I experienced a feeling, not unlike that of a twisted ankle, which was no surprise as I *had* twisted my ankle and which now found me stumbling round in the pitch black like something from Monty Python's, Ministry of Silly Walks whilst 'squealing like a stuck pig!' as they say in some southern US states. But it wasn't until the next morning when the alcohol had worn off, that it was to become clear how bad it was. It was at this point that Sam finally started to find the proceedings amusing.

Chapter 4
Edale to Crowden

Day 1

Distance 15 mls
Total 15 mls

It was early again when I emerged from my nice, warm, comfortable, duvet enshrouded slumber to be met by murky, overcast, drizzling skies. Not a good start to the day I thought? Something else which signified it wasn't going to be a good day was when I tried to get out of bed and stand up for I suddenly found myself falling in a starboard direction (that's right for you non-navigational types). This was accompanied by a re-occurrence of the pain I felt the night before and confirmed that which I'd hoped was just a figment of my imagination or the result of an alcohol-induced nightmare – my ankle was well and truly bloody sprained! Was this an omen I pondered? A message from the Gods? A warning to give up now perhaps? No, it was justice for being an annoying drunken prat! But I was determined I wasn't going to give up a second time so just viewed this to be a sign of weakness on the part of my right foot. It had decided to chicken out after coming all this way but, as they came in a pair and the left one was still as willing as I, it was out-voted. Not only that but sod it! I thought I couldn't again face the ridicule from my workmates who found it highly amusing the last time I failed, and I certainly wasn't going back to face the wife who had already accused me of plunging us into debt with my antics. Unfortunately, her misgivings were to be proved right for a lot of promised work was lost during the time I was away, leaving me with a £700 black hole in my tax account!

To placate my dissenting ankle, I wrapped two bandages around it and placed it in a pair of thick socks, but it could still be heard whining and moaning. Soon though it would be in a boot, a stout leather boot from which no amount of whimpering could emanate. On noticing my obvious hobbled descent of the stairs I was met with the immediate sympathy you would expect from a valued friend. It was sometime before Sam gained control of himself and wiped away the tears, and, after the sounds of convulsed laughter had stopped echoing around the walls, he offered some words that did little to comfort me.

"It was your own bloody fault!" he said. "If you hadn't buggered about it wouldn't have happened!"

Had Sam been on that ill-fated Antarctic expedition of 1912 when Captain Oates sacrificed himself after uttering those immortal words,

"I am just going outside and may be some time."

Sam would probably have replied,

"Well make sure you close the bloody flap on your way out!"

With his biting words to console me, I limped into the kitchen and cried into my eggy soldiers.

Breakfast over I added another bandage to my ever enlarging ankle, a handful of painkillers to my nervous system and donned my boots ready for the off. Unfortunately, I had forgotten about the small rock face that needed scaling outside the back door and approached it with some trepidation, preparing myself for an abseiling attempt. But I was surprised to find that it wasn't anywhere near as high this morning as it had seemed in my drunken stupor the night before?

We left Ringinglow around 8.30 for the half hour drive to Edale, the apprehensive starting point when walking north and the celebratory finishing point when coming south. Nothing much was said on the drive except for me grizzling about how unfair life is etc, etc. You've probably gathered by now that I'm one of life's pessimists. I'm also, according to my wife and kids, a boring old fart, which is probably a truer description. I tend to think of myself more as a loner. I hate crowds, even small groups of people I can only tolerate for a short length of time, which is why the Penning Way appealed to me so strongly. For two whole weeks, I was going to have solitude and peace and walk through some of the most secluded, isolated, remote countryside in Britain. Instead of screaming kids it will be the cry of nature; the refuse and litter of the streets will be replaced by natures own wastage; the only noise will be the sound of a running stream or the breeze urging me along and human contact will be minimal.

We picked up the A625 at Hathersage which we followed for about four miles before turning off at the village of Hope for the final five-mile drive to Edale. Ever since leaving Hathersage we had been accompanied by the peaceful river Noe which has its origins in the Vale of England and which, with the sun now breaking through the clouds, looked inviting enough to make you want to sit by its lazy banks all day while recounting past pleasant moments of your childhood. We turned off up the narrow lane that winds its way under the railway bridge, past the Y.H.A. and the tourist information centre before coming to the kick-off point for all P.W. walkers: The Nags Head Inn. Here I debussed gingerly from the car, grabbed my rucksack and joined the queue. "What queue?" I hear you ask. Well, any and everybody who walks the Way has to have the obligatory photo taken outside the pub to at least prove that they made it that far; and this morning was no exception. Being a Saturday it was probably more busy than normal as some walkers come just for the weekend or one day for the attempt on Kinder Scout or many of the other walks that start from Edale. Some just come for the photo, perhaps as a reminder of something they'd like to do but can't or won't ever get the chance to. Others may be to rekindle happy memories of something they once did but were never likely to repeat. I was going to suggest a 'snake' queuing system, as they have in post offices, with two separate emplacements for photo's; one for the day-trippers, general sightseers and members of the Pennine Way appreciation society; and one for the genuine P.W. endeavourers. But the queue would probably foul up the traffic in Sheffield!

Pictures taken I said my goodbyes to Sam and was just about to launch into the old "If I don't make it back," speech before I realised the sort of reaction I'd get from him, and I'd already had enough derision for one day. So I just bade him farewell and limped off up the lane to join the path. To make sure there were no navigational errors this time I checked and rechecked my map, took several compass bearings, re-read Wainwright's book, noted the azimuth of the sun in relation to the topography of the land, then, to be on the safe side, followed the little wooden sign that said '**Pennine Way →**' I just hope they've remembered to put those every 100yards?

The first obstacle met is the narrow, wooden bridge that crosses Grindsbrook and, having successfully conquered it, was considering resting up and having a well-earned cup of tea, but seeing as I had only been walking for 2 mins I thought it best I push on a bit further? The sun was up and the weather warm, so I stripped down to my T-shirt before beginning the steep ascent up Grindsbrook to reach Kinder Scout. Even after a short distance, it was obvious that my ankle was not going to ease off and my limp became quite pronounced. So much so that other walkers overtaking my laboured efforts kept asking if I was OK and suggested I turn back. To combat this constant assault on my physical ability, let alone sanity, I would sit down every time another backpacker neared feigning exhaustion, although some of it wasn't contrived. Once they passed I would hobble on again for another few yards. This proved to be an extremely slow way of progressing, combined with having to criss-cross Grindsbrook time and time again, rock scrambling in some places.

Eventually, I made it to the top of the climb, breathless but relieved that my ankle had made it this far, although the rest of me was still trying to catch up. Behind me was the steep descent back to civilisation and real ale. What lay before me was the gooey, black morass of Kinder Scout. The pint was more enticing but would have to wait.

The view down Grindsbrook

The view from the top of Grindsbrook across the plateau was quite something or probably would have been as I couldn't see much due to the mist that had descended. It was at this point that I made a stupid mistake. Instead of taking a compass bearing from here towards Kinder Downfall, I decided to walk to a group of rocks I thought was Crowden Head and take bearings from there. This was not an easy task as Kinder Scout consists mainly of groughs, sort of trenches where the peat has eroded. These can be up to ten feet deep in places with no assurances of having a firm base to them once descended into. Trying to climb back out was even more of an ordeal! On reaching the outcrop of rocks I realised I wasn't where I thought I was and now it was too far to hobble back to the start again, so I decided to continue in the general direction of River Kinder hoping to pick up a rivulet that I could follow. For some reason, I just happened to glance back over my shoulder back towards where I'd just been (wherever that was?) and noticed about half a dozen other walkers who appeared likewise lost and had decided that I looked like I knew where I was going, and so had elected to follow me! Not wanting to be responsible for the untimely demise of several other lost souls, I opted for a game of Kinder Scout hide-and-seek. This entailed me limping casually across the top of the moor as if I had a purpose and then quickly dropping down into a peat grough where I would hobble as fast as my ankle would allow in a completely different direction, occasionally popping my head up to see the others running round like headless chickens wondering where I was going to emerge next?

After a couple of hours, I eventually came across a small trickle of water that seemed to be flowing in the right direction and followed it for a while before coming to Kinder Gates, a rock formation that the river flows between as it wends its way to emerge finally at Kinder Downfall.

Unfortunately, due to the lack of rain that had been experienced over the last couple of years, there wasn't the expected deluge of water the gives the downfall its name, instead there was a small dribble that sort of clung to the rocks as if afraid of heights before finally letting go and continuing on down to Kinder Reservoir. In wetter and windier times this downfall is actually blown back up vertically!

The mist had now lifted and afforded me views westward towards Stockport. I rested for a quick 15mins to give my ankle a breather before I realised that the Kinder 'posse' might catch up with me soon and may want me to guide them for the rest of the walk, so on I marched; albeit lopsidedly.

My next destination was Mill Hill where I chanced upon a lady Park Warden who, noticing the obvious reluctance of my right foot to keep in step with the left, inquired as to whether I thought I was doing the right thing and did I want her to look at it? Had she said 'Would you like to come home with me so that I can soothe and massage your aching and broken body?' then I probably would have taken her up on it. But instead, I straightened my shoulders, puffed out my chest, put on my best macho face, declined her offer, thanked her for her concern and limped off resolutely – down the wrong path. This I realised after about 30yds, and, not wanting to embarrass myself even further, decided to sit down on the grass for a few minutes gazing at the flora and fauna as if that was my intention all along, eventually returning to the correct path up to Mill Hill after she'd gone.

The trudge over Featherbed Moss was worse than the last time I attempted it, being one endless stream of peat groughs, and I found myself quite frequently sinking up to my knees in sticky, smelly, thick, black/brown gunge. To those of you not familiar with either peat or groughs please let me explain. Firstly – peat: Described by those that know as, "Semi carbonised vegetable matter formed by partial decomposition in water of various plants, esp. mosses of the genus *Sphagnum*". I prefer my description. Secondly – groughs: These are basically weaknesses in the peat where water either runs or collects and can vary in depth and width from a few inches to around 10 feet. Add the two together and you have a very efficient way of trapping passing backpackers who, if not rescued in a day or two, will, themselves, also become decomposing vegetable matter. I must have added another two miles to the days walking just trying to find ways around the groughs, but in places, there was no way around and it meant me having to jump them, which did my ankle a world of good. Not! The marvellous thing about being in such a desolate place is that nobody can hear you scream, which was a blessing and meant that I could keep my pride intact.

Featherbed Moss and Bleaklow Head, the next destination, have two things in common with each other. They are both covered in peat and they are both extremely boring unless you have a fascination for peat that is? To reach Bleaklow Head you first have to cross the A57 Snake Pass, which, as every good motorist knows, is normally the first road in Britain to be closed every year come winter. As the cuckoo heralds the first breaths of spring, so the closure of Snakes Pass signals the demise of autumn, and, at 1680ft above sea level, I'm not surprised? Once crossed you are faced with a boggy walk up Devil's Dyke. No Devil – all Dyke. This is reached after crossing Doctors' Gate. No Doctor – no Gate. And thence up onto Bleaklow Head. No head – not low – very bleak! From the summit, it's all downhill to Crowden, and this year I managed to descend down the right side of Wildboar Grain! In so doing I came across two Mancurians listening intently to a portable radio to the last 15mins of a Man Utd V Arsenal F.A. Cup match. Those footie fanatics amongst you will be able to tell me exactly what year it was, what day, what time and probably my true navigational position relative to the Arsenal defensive line up?

The final drop down to Reaps Farm is very steep, long and uneven and not the best terrain for a sprained ankle, so it was a case of bite the bullet time if I wanted to make any headway. Eventually, I made it to the A628 and decided to follow the road until I came to the front entrance of the campsite rather than carry on along the P.W., which skirts Highstones Hill behind the site before dropping down into it. This was to make it easier on my ankle and, considering I walked that bit last year, I didn't feel I was cheating, which made it easier on my conscience too.

Crowden campsite hadn't changed one iota since the last time I visited, which wasn't surprising as it was only last year? But there was something missing this time. Midges! The previous year I was inundated with millions of the little buggers and there was nowhere to hide! Meals had to be eaten alfresco under a towel-draped head because to try and conceal yourself inside your tent was made impossible due to the fact that, like every good restaurant, the best tables had already gone, albeit to a host of tiny, unrelenting, greedy little flesh biting insects! But this year was different. There was not one midge to be found anywhere, not even one diehard still hovering around the dustbins. Nothing! I came to the conclusion that having set upon the hapless campers en-masse the year before, they obviously thought that nobody would be stupid enough to try for a return visit. Fortunately, they didn't bargain on this idiot!

After setting up camp I headed for the comfort of a hot shower. This helped soothe my aches and pains and made the day seem not so bad on reflection. I limped back to my tent refreshed, wrapped my ankle in a cold-soaked bandage and lay for what seemed an age in the warm, midge-free, sunny evening's sultriness. To soothe my mind I listened to some classical music on my tiny radio while I filled in my diary and checked tomorrow's route, eventually turning in around 9 pm for what I hoped would be a quiet night's sleep. What I hoped for and what I got were two entirely different things?

What I hadn't banked on was the militant wing of Insomniacs Anonymous holding one of their nocturnal gatherings to compare the musical attributes of their numerous car horns. This started around 2 am and continued intermittently until about 6 am, and consisted of two or three cars parked somewhere outside the site, but obviously close enough, blaring their horns in no set musical format or tempo for around 10-15mins and then leaving it for about half hour to lure you into a false sense of slumber before starting again. I was probably thinking the same as all the other campers in that somebody else will probably go and tell them to bugger off, so there was no point in two of us getting cold, so I stayed inside my nice warm sleeping bag. Eventually, it did stop but by then sleep was impossible. When I enquired at the camp shop the next morning as to what it was all about I was told ominously that "It was being taken care of!" So I left it at that.

Chapter 5
Crowden to Standedge

Day 2

Distance 12 mls
Total 27mls

The morning was how a Sunday should be, sunny and peaceful with just a hint of lethargy in the air and, by the time breakfast was taken care of, all thoughts of last night's musical rendition of 'Just a Horn at Twilight' had all but faded. My ankle had now subsided from the barrage balloon it had been the night before but was still reluctant to join the rest of my body in today's little jaunt. It was while breakfasting that I noticed two army-type persons emerging from a tent just over from me and assumed they were trying to do the walk the hardest way possible due to some military gauntlet being thrown down, possibly by another squad or their commanding officer.

It was while I was packing up my gear that these two gentlemen approached me and enquired about the size of my tent, or lack of it, and how I'd managed to stow everything inside my rucksack? I must admit to feeling quite chuffed that two of Her Majesties finest who had probably spent more time 'under canvas' in every conceivable location, terrain and climate imaginable, were actually asking me, a lowly backpacker, the ins'-and-outs' on the best lightweight equipment to buy? So, not one to deprive others of my experience, even if somewhat limited, I started to pour forth earnestly what little I did know and told them about my tent being a Saunders JetPacker Plus which, at 3lb 12oz, was one of the lightest on the market. I then went on to extol the virtues of my Karrimor E63 rucksack; my Epigas demountable stove; my Field & Trek four season sleeping bag; Zamberlain all-leather boots; Silva compass; Footprint maps; Olympus camera etc, etc. It was after about 15mins that I noticed that they had slowly inched their way back to their tent and were gradually edging themselves inside, obviously under the impression they had chanced upon a backpacking version of a train-spotter and working on the assumption that if they ignored me I would probably go away. This was the desired effect I was after due to the fact that my intention was to do the Way as a solo effort and not to team up with others who will have their own targets to accomplish and times to do it in.

Having safely seen off any chance of unwanted company I quickly finished packing and departed from the campsite via the rear entrance that leads back up onto Highstones Hill. From here the path winds its way precariously along Laddow Rocks. I say precariously because in places the path comes within a foot or two of the edge and if concentration or surefootedness isn't observed, you could find yourself plummeting nearly 200ft to your untimely demise, as the carcasses of many dead sheep bared witness to. Once Crowden Great Brook is reached the terrain flattens out somewhat, if only for a short period before starting its long gradual climb up to Black Hill.

Torside reservoir, Crowden

It was while filling my water bottle from one of the many small tributaries that run down off the fells into the brook that another solitary walker caught up with me and started to pass the time of day and enquired if I minded some companionship. At first, obviously for the reasons already stated, I was somewhat reluctant to accept his offer, but then he assured me he was only doing a round walk from

Crowden up to Black Hill and then back down Heydon Clough, so I agreed, mainly because it would help take my mind off my ankle, which was in full voice this morning. We talked about nothing in particular for the first 2½mls but it made the time fly past and gave me a chance to think about something other than my injury. We finally reached the summit and it immediately became obvious why it was named Black Hill. The only thing up here that wasn't black was the trig point, which gleamed pure white in a sea of ebony morass. Today we were lucky in-as-much as the going was firm and you only sank up to your knees if you walked in the wrong places, where, as it is said among backpackers of old, that most times of the year you have to swim to the trig point! Even old Wainwright himself had to be extricated from here by his walking companion and a passing warden because he sank up to his waist when he tried to approach the summit.

I was just about to say goodbye to my short-lived friend when he produced a flask and enquired as to whether I fancied a nice cup of Earl Grey tea. The answer was obviously in the affirmative. It's a funny thing, but offer an Englishman a cup of tea in any situation, be it in a foxhole under fire or stranded in the middle of the jungle after having survived a plane crash, and for those few minutes, everything's alright with the world. He can be on his last legs dragging himself through Death Valley, but offer him a nice cup of tea and it will cheer him up no end. This was no exception. On the exposed, barren summit of Black Hill, a nice, hot, steaming cup of Earl Grey went down a treat and set me up for the rest of the day.

I finally bade him goodbye and was just about to depart when who should appear but our two military backpackers who surprisingly made a beeline straight for me and enquired how I was doing, having noticed my labouring lower limb. A conversation was struck up and names were exchanged; theirs being Barry and Kevin, who were both from Kent, and, with me heralding from Essex, we felt a sort of southern comradeship with all three of us feeling lonely and vulnerable being this far north of Watford. We decided to walk together for the rest of the day as I already knew the route from last year, even though then I took the wrong one, ending up on the Wessenden alternative. I wasn't going to make that same mistake again. So I read my compass, took my bearing, ignored the marker posts I followed last time and we all trudged off across Wessenden Head Moor towards the A635 on the official path.

This turned out to be just another expanse of endless peat groughs with no hint of whether we were heading in the right direction or not and meant working solely on compass bearings. Now, this may be a simple act on flat, open ground, but when you have to keep varying your course to negotiate the groughs, unless you have a landmark to aim for it's an impossible task to keep on your bearing. Fortunately, we chanced upon a middle-aged couple coming in the other direction who pointed out that if I looked really hard towards the horizon we should just be able to make out a marker post. And lo, we did look hard, we looked very, very hard indeed, and in the fullness of time I spied yonder post, but only because I was wearing glasses. From this distance, the way-marker looked like a slightly taller blade of grass in the middle of Wembley football pitch! Once I found it I dared not take my eyes off it otherwise I would never find it again.

We finally made the A635 and were rewarded with a cup of tea and a burger at the van that plies its trade on this stretch. It was sad to think that less than a mile down the road was the infamous Saddleworth Moor, known more for its connection with the Bodies on the Moors murders than its desolate beauty. Being such an isolated spot it's understandable to see how easy it was to dispose of bodies knowing that the odds of them being found were next to impossible.

Nourished, we pushed on, first over White Moss then Black Moss, (personally I couldn't tell the difference, but then I'd led a sheltered life), before meeting up with the end point of the Wessenden alternative at Black Moss reservoir.

This, like all the other reservoirs I was to come across, was extremely low for this time of year. All-in-all, a bad sign.

It transpired in the course of walking that Barry and Kevin were actually civilian police-dog handlers at a military base and not actually military persons as I had earlier thought, which now explains why the lack of knowledge as regards camping equipment and somewhat dampened my ego as regards educating what I thought were two hardened, fighting men. But, like all good security personnel, they declined to talk any further on their work, so we changed the subject. The last 1½mls down to Globe Hill Farm at Standedge went without incident and we arrived there at about 4 pm in glorious sunshine, which had eluded us for most of the day, finally showing itself about half hour before we finished. We all threw our gear down and collapsed; me because of my ankle and Kevin from a painful knee, which had started playing up just after Black Hill. Once rested we erected tents, removed offending foot ware, showered (separately) and were then treated at the farm to a satisfying meal of egg, sausage, chips, bread & butter, apple pie & custard, all washed down with copious amounts of tea. This was all followed by a laze in the afternoon sun while waiting for the pub down the road to open. While we were laying there two other guys turned up who were also walking the Way, but they were doing it for charity. I had considered this myself but dismissed it on the grounds of selfishness. I wanted to do this for me and not feel that I was letting anybody else down if I failed, plus sometimes you can push yourself too far in the name of charity and do serious bodily harm. This was borne out by the fact that one of these guys had badly blistered feet due to borrowing somebody else's boots because he didn't have any of his own, and too many people were relying on him to do it. As a matter of fact, on removing his boots his right foot was just one big plaster and I pondered on whether he was actually being sponsored by Elastoplast.

It was while talking to the lady of the farm that we were told of a middle-aged gentleman that, up to that point, had actually walked the Pennine Way six times in all and was considering becoming a guide for parties of people wishing to experience it. No doubt that record has now been bettered, along with the record held by a man who ran it in under three days, and another who walked the whole route carrying everything in a plastic carrier bag. Records were the furthest thing from my mind at the moment, I just wanted to complete it once and do it in one piece.

Just before moseying down to the pub I decided to make full use of the warm evening sun and wash my smalls, as well as my bigs, ready for tomorrow in case I didn't get the chance for another couple of days. This done, I hung them out on a makeshift line to dry in the warmth of the evening. It was now supping time, something I'd looked forward to for the last two days because the pub had everything I wanted; real ale, old décor, quiet company, and, best of all, Glenn Miller playing on an old Bakelite radio sitting on the bar. This was obviously wired up to a cassette player somewhere hidden unless the rumours about him still being alive were true and he was doing Sunday night stints in a pub in Yorkshire so he could pay his Poll Tax?

Murky view of White Hill from Standedge

Unfortunately, I had to limit myself to 2½ pints; firstly because I didn't fancy the idea of dragging myself from my tent every half hour during the night to answer the call of nature; and secondly, because I didn't want to wake up the next morning with a hangover. We arrived back at about 9.30 where I then found to my dismay that my clothes were nowhere near dry and, with a damp evening forecast, couldn't see any chance of them being so by the morning. This would leave me with the problem of carrying a rucksack full of wet clothes, practically doubling the weight and worsening my ankle. But that's tomorrow's problem, for now, I'll have to sleep on it and see what happens in the morning.

Chapter 6
Standedge to Colden

Day 3

Distance 17mls
Total 44mls

A suggestion was put forward by Mr Elastoplast that was met with open arms by the others and trepidation by me, that being that we send our equipment onto the next campsite by taxi to give us an easy days walking. At first, I objected on the grounds that I wanted to do the Pennine Way with all its problems and hardships, whatever they were. But on giving it some careful consideration I realised that if I didn't give my ankle at least one day's easy hiking then I probably wouldn't last the rest of the walk anyway, especially with my rucksack having the weight of a small reservoir due to my washed clothes still being fairly damp in the morning. So this agreed we booked the taxi, took what we needed, left our gear with the owners of the site and sauntered off up the track to rejoin the path up on Standedge, the walking plaster having left some half hour before Barry, Kevin and myself.

The views from here were stunning. Looking S.W. you were afforded excellent views of Oldham in all its grotesque glory and, with the sun already high and hot, the mist that covered Greater Manchester would soon be burnt off to leave the sprawling mass exposed for all to see, not that anybody would want to unless you were on the brink of suicide and you needed just one more reason to justify your termination. About a mile further on we came upon an experimental path that was in the process of being laid. This consisted of a man-made membrane on which different layers of ever-increasing sized gravel were laid with the intention of, if the information board that was erected was to be believed, the surrounding grasses eventually growing over and through the gravel so that after a time the path would appear natural. It was less a case of 'follow the yellow brick road' and more a case of 'follow the grey/black, shingle encrusted, totally unnatural, man-made concourse'. So, just like the Lion, the Tin Man and the Scarecrow, we followed the said path.

We eventually emerged at the A640 and were just about to cross the road when, for no apparent reason, Kevin's nose started bleeding? Perhaps it was the altitude? My First Aid training came into its own here and I soon had the little bleeder under control, although what caused it we had no idea? We pushed on over Reaps Hill and White Hill, (another misnomer), and headed towards the T.V. mast on Windy Hill, which wasn't a misnomer at all. In fact, it was a very apt description of the place and one which I kept telling the others about as we got nearer and nearer having experienced it the year prior. Just before the T.V. mast we came across another burger van and, not wishing to upset the economy of the northern industrial regions, we opted for a cuppa and a burger and were told that our two friends had passed this way about half hour hence, which meant they were making good time, considering mateys infirmity.

Our thirst quenched and our hunger abated I warned them to brace themselves against the power of the gales about to strike them as we approached the mast. Imagine how stupid I felt when we got there and there wasn't even a draught!

"But I swear," I protested, "the last time I was here it took all of my strength just to keep upright!"

Kevin and Barry just looked at me, nodded and kept on walking. I felt not unlike a fool. A few yards further on found us standing on the specially built footbridge that spans the M62, looking down on the constant, never-ending stream of noisy, air polluting cars and lorries that criss-cross the Trans-Pennine route 24 hours a day, 365 days a year. I began to wonder how many of those drivers, with no real destination in life, were looking up envious of our escapism, while we looked down with nothing but contempt for the rat-race in all its glory. Fortunately, this was one of the last points along the walk where we encountered traffic in any sort of abundance and could look forward to quieter days ahead.

Footbridge over M62

The approach to Blackstone Edge was long but not too arduous and afforded clear views back towards Black Hill some ten miles distant. It was while on the path leading to the summit that we spied what looked like stones that had been arranged in strange patterns. Maybe it was Devil worshipers we thought? Or perhaps some sort of Pagan ritual had been performed here? It wasn't until we were right on top of them that I realised they were spelling out a profound message which read "FUCK THE POLL TAX" The problem being that it could only really be seen with any clarity from the air, which posed the question that maybe it was intended for the eyes of the Air Transport minister, or any Tory MP that just happened to be flying overhead.

We pushed on from Blackstone Edge and, due to the steep incline, were forced to break into a trot or fast hobble in my case. This nearly met with some disaster when we ran, literally, into a group of school kids on a day trip to the countryside. The little angels had decided to do their very best to get in our way and make it as awkward as possible for us to pass. Fortunately their teacher sensed our determination to reach our objective whatever the cost and instructed the fiends to "Stand to one side and let the gentlemen pass," knowing that if he didn't he'd have to go back to school and try to explain to the irate parents why so many children in his care were in hospital with multiple fractures.

A few minutes later we reached the point where I had given up last year, the White Horse Inn. This time though I kept walking straight past and continued down the track along Blackstone Edge reservoir, occasionally looking back with a feeling of triumph. To think that the last time I gave up it was because of small blisters on my toes and here I was with not only a sprained ankle but also a large blister on the back of my left heel with not a thought of defeat. Although the walk was by no means over, I felt I had already beaten it!

We carried on past Light Hazzels and Warland reservoirs, all the time following the rough sand/gravel track that runs alongside them until we emerged once more onto the normal grass path. From here our next objective stood out quite clearly on the horizon two miles further on, that being the 120ft obelisk of Stoodley Pike. For some strange reason, Barry, who had been taking constant compass bearings along the route to make sure we didn't go astray, decided to take a reading for the monument, even though we could clearly see it and the path that ran straight up to the door of the thing! Kevin just looked at me and shook his head as if to say "Let him get on with it, it makes him happy." We finally made it to Stoodley Pike without a bearing, tracker dogs or guide and climbed the pitch-black interior steps that led to a balcony where the whole of the surrounding hills could be surveyed. This, coupled with the blazing sunshine, seemed to make all the aches, pains and blisters worthwhile.

Stoodly Pike

As a bit of history for those interested. Stoodley Pike was built in 1814 to commemorate the peace of Ghent and the abdication of Napoleon, and there's not a lot of people know that!

After a brief respite, we moved off to enjoy a very pleasant stroll down through the leafy gladded birch trees of Callis Wood on a path that wove back and forth until finally emerging at the Rochdale Canal. The dirty Rochdale Canal. The dirty, smelly

Rochdale Canal. It was a depressing end to a fine picturesque descent. From nature as it should be to man as he'll always be. We quickly crossed the road, not wanting to stay any longer than we had to, and, after passing under an old brick railway arch, we had the chance to prove beyond a reasonable doubt the reversal theory of Newton's law of gravity that states that everything that comes down, must go up. In this case, the thing was us and the up was the very steep climb up to Pry Hill. It started off as a road and quickly turned into a cobbled track which wove between old houses and cottages before coming to a section where you could either continue on the official PW path or try the Wainwright alternative. Needless to say, Barry wanted to go for the alternative, and, seeing as how we were making good time, Kevin and I agreed.

The path should have been a small detour deviating only by half a mile, but the signs were few and far between and seemed to point through people's gardens rather than fields. An hour later we managed to find the true path and carry on as we initially intended, finally reaching Colden totally knackered. We strolled up to our supposed night's stay, which was an iffy looking pub in the village, but couldn't find anybody in, which was a little disturbing as our gear was supposed to have been left here. We finally found our rucksacks in an outside shed with no lock on the door, which I found worrying, to say the least. But on reflection, I realised this was rural Yorkshire and not London. Here you could still leave your back door unlocked with no concern of anybody entering your home. Whereas in London, you'd be lucky to return to still find the door! On closer examination of the surrounding area of the pub, the only field we could find to camp in was knee deep in thistles and covered in sheep. So, after a hasty conference, we pushed on for *my* original intended night's stay which was only another two miles further on. By this time the other two lads had appeared, having found a pub en-route and had been testing its waters for impurities. All five of us pressed on for High Greenwood House, tonight's camp, in the hope that it turns out better than the pub grounds. Once again Barry excelled himself by asking everybody he came across if we were on the right path for the site, which was painfully obvious as the path led nowhere else except straight for it!

We arrived exhausted but happy, having completed 17 miles with dodgy ankles, swollen knees and blistered feet. With the sun still beating down as it had done most of the day, we erected tents, fed stomachs and showered bodies. I managed to rig up another makeshift clothesline and hung my still damp belongings out to dry, but had to keep a watchful eye on them due to a nosey calf that kept trying to eat them through the fence. Fed and refreshed, we all tended blisters and sprains, powdered feet and set to talking about tomorrows walking. This proved to be a bone of contention because I'd made up my mind that I wanted to go back to my solo effort. My planning had allowed for a good 25 miles walking to reach the next day's objective, Gargrave, and to make up for some of the shorter days walking I had done at the beginning. But on hearing this, Barry argued that Kevin's knee probably wouldn't last that far and we should aim for something shorter.

"Good point," I said, "But that's what I had planned for tomorrow."

"But?" protested Barry, "it's too far for Kevin to walk?"

"I know," I agreed, "But if I have any chance of finishing the walk in two weeks then I'd have to reach Gargrave tomorrow to be on schedule." Barry continued.

"But there's no way Kevin could last that far. Maybe we should aim for something shorter?"

"Well you can, but I need to press on."

"But I think we should all stick together?"

I was now beginning to lose my patience and replied rather tersely; "Look, that's tomorrow's destination as far as I'm concerned! I've spent years planning the route and I've got it all worked out where I should be and when, so the best thing is that you aim for your target and I'll aim for mine and hopefully we'll see each other at the finish. OK?"

Barry finally realised that this was the parting of the ways and slunk off sulking. We all turned in for the night early, wishing each other well for the next day and good luck for the rest of the walk. I went to sleep a happy man knowing that I'd finally got rid of them and could get back to some peaceful, if not sane walking.

Looking back towards Stoodley Pike

Chapter 7
Colden to Gargrave

Day 4

Distance 16mls
Total 70mls

It was about 5 am when I awoke, surrounded by the sounds of broken bodies groaning inside comfortable warm sleeping bags, apprehensive at what the day waited to throw at them. We said our good mornings somewhat reservedly through nylon walls and I set about the daily bodily routine of checking that all the relevant bits were still there and in good working order, and then conducted a group therapy session with the outer limbs and internal organs to persuade them that they were doing the right thing and that the day would soon be over if they just all pulled together and humoured the idiot who thought up the idea. All major areas were placated until I got to the right ankle, who was still sulking at not being taken any notice of from day one, and who had now proceeded to inflate itself again until I paid attention and saw reason.

I was hoping to be first away that morning as I had furthest to go, but the others decided to skip breakfast and consequently departed some 30 mins before me. Fortunately, my clothes were now dry except for my corduroy trousers, which I had placed underneath my bedroll, sandwiched between sheets of newspaper in a last-ditched attempt at drying them. In the end, I had to settle instead for wearing them damp so as to dry them off as I walked. I finally broke camp at 6.30, which was half an hour later than I wanted, and meant I'd have to get my head down and cover some ground if I wanted to finish the day on time.

The weather was dry with an early morning mist that seemed to exaggerate every little birdcall and leaf rustle and gave me an eerie feeling of total loneliness as if nothing else existed outside the enshrouding fog. This feeling was soon shattered when a young lad looking no more than 15, screamed past me on his moped, which sounded more like a castrated wasp than a motorbike. By the time I reached the Walshaw Dean reservoir, the mist had lifted and the sun shone through, which meant I could abandon my sweatshirt and body warmer and get down to some serious walking.

Having tracks to walk on made life a damn sight easier and helped to make up the time, but this didn't seem to help the famous four who I could see quite clearly up ahead and who were only about a mile further on. Considering they left half an hour before me, they should have been at least 2-2½mls further on? Anyhow, I was left with a serious decision to make. Should I slow down and hang back in case I catch up with them and make it the famous five again? Or should I just go for broke and try to overtake them, hoping to out-pace them? In the end, I decided that if I was going to make good time then I had better get stuck in and damn the consequences!

About half an hour later saw me emerge onto Withens Height, which turned out to be just another recruiting ground for Peat Boggers Anonymous. The only difference here was that 'duckboards' had been laid as a walking aid. Funny thing was that not one solitary duck could be seen anywhere, which is indicative of the animal kingdom. I can't remember the last time I saw a Zebra using a crossing? Or a Birdie playing golf? Or a Panda driving a police car? (you have to be over a certain age to know that one). I reached the end of the duck-less boards and stepped back onto the familiar non-existence of terra firma, otherwise known as peatus boggus. Unfortunately, this peatus boggus had the consistency of three-week-old porridge, which only became evident when I tried the inherent bodily movement known as walking. All systems in the body were in agreement as regards the neuromuscular process needed to carry out said manoeuvre, and did so to the best of their ability. The head moved forward to begin momentum; the torso leant past the angle of balance to facilitate a pulling action on the legs; and the thigh muscles and buttocks initiated the stepping action.

Unfortunately, though, my feet were stuck fast in the porridge. This ended a perfectly fluid linear motion in a not so perfect horizontal finish. None of this was helped by the 50lb rucksack clinging like a limpet mine to my back. The result being that I ended up elbow deep in said porridge! Slowly, I dragged myself out of the quagmire and, looking like a throwback from the Black and White Minstrel Show (ask your Dad), proceeded to try and clean myself up. The only problem was that all I could find within arm's reach without covering everything in peat was my handkerchief which, by the time I'd finished with it, looked more like a year-old floor-cloth, and one which I had no intention of ever blowing my nose on again? So I can reveal for the first time dear reader, that somewhere in a dry stonewall up on Withens Height, there is concealed a dirty, peat-infested handkerchief, hopefully in the latter stages of decay.

A stone's throw further on is Top Withens, reputed to be the site of Wuthering Heights in Emily Bronte's book of the same name. But a plaque on the ruined building states that there is no connection whatsoever and, never having read the book, I couldn't argue the fact one way or another. The only comment I can make is about the views. If this is where Ms Bronte spent her time writing and gathering inspiration for her books, then she deserved every penny of her royalties. For although it is a desolate and lonely place, the panorama, on a clear day like today, was breathtaking, even if I didn't know what I was looking at due to the information on my maps being limited to about ¼ mile either side of the Pennine Way.

Plaque at Top Withens

After the customary photo's I pushed on down towards Ponden reservoir only to be met at the bottom by the four musketeers, who were looking decidedly knackered. I enquired as to why they were not a good 2-3mls ahead of me and was told that Barry had been navigating and had led them completely down the wrong path which they didn't realise until they had reached the bottom of a hill and which meant they had to climb all the way back up again, hence the reason for their exhausted disposition. I quickly seized the opportunity and, while practically at a limping-run, informed them that I would like to stay and chat but with a long journey ahead of me I'd better keep going. I left them in a cloud of dust not daring to look back in case they were trying to attract my attention in the hope of talking me into walking with them, which would be understandable with Barry having the navigation skills of a headless chicken.

The path from the reservoir up to Wolf Stones was extremely steep and tiring and at one point I had to knock at a cottage for a top up to my water bottle because there was no indication of a waterhole for at least another five miles, and I was already down to less than half-full. The lady who answered the door was understandably apprehensive at having a stranger visit her in the middle of the day and eyed me very suspiciously. I had to put on my best southern accent and behaviour to win her over and convince her I wasn't a wild man of the woods or a vagrant, although standing there with four days stubble and covered in peat from my earlier experience, I wasn't too convinced myself?

It was about noon when I reached the town of Ickornshaw and was feeling decidedly peckish. So, after descending a very steep bank which led down to what could best be described as the High Street, I enquired of a passing local tradesman if there were any cafes or fish & chip shops where I could satisfy my hunger pains. I was pointed in the direction of the Black Bull public house which, unfortunately, was situated back up the top of the very steep bank which, now I was looking up, seemed more in line with an Alpine climb than a footpath for backpackers. But, considering what was at the top the ascent, it was well worth it. After first making myself presentable with a quick visit to the loo, I returned to feast heartily on steak and kidney pie with chips and mushy peas, washed down with two pints of lemonade. I was just in the process of selecting a sweet when the now familiar sounds of Barry and his merry men came drifting through from the pub car park. By the time they fell through the door and into the bar I was already packed and on my way out, just staying long enough to pay the bill and wish them good walking, and then I was gone. I decided to increase my limp and put some miles between us in case they cut short their lunch in the hope of catching up with me again.

From Ickornshaw to Thornton-in-Craven was easy going and uneventful, which basically means I can't remember anything about it? The weather up to this point had been quite warm and dry, but by the time I'd reached the Leeds-Liverpool canal the heavens opened, which seemed wasted as there was already enough water in the channel? A couple of hundred yards further on I passed under the double arched bridge at East Marton, which has defied explanation as to its construction. I can only assume that someone in the civil engineering department of the municipal council was studying the drawings after a rather lengthy Friday lunch-time session in the local Duck and Fleece and decided that if it was two bridges he could see on the plans, then two bridges they were going to get? Who was he to argue?

Double arched bridge at East Marton

Between the bridge and the day's final resting place three miles away, Gargrave, it chucked it down non-stop and, due to the still warm temperatures, I got just as soaked inside my cagoule from sweat as I did outside from the rain. So, all in all, wearing my waterproofs was a bloody waste of time!

I finally trickled into Gargrave at around 5.30 after walking for almost 11 hours with only a short break and made straight for the campsite, which I knew the location of from having stayed in a cottage in the town a couple of years before. By this time the rain had stopped falling and my body had stopped melting and, after a good hot shower, I hit the local chippie. Boy, two fish & chip meals in one day? I knew how to live! Once replenished I did have the intention of walking along the canal to a pub called the Anchor but decided I'd already done enough for one day and retired to my tent to recuperate instead. The last time I was here I remember stopping in at the Anchor because of a sign outside that said they sold good old Tetley's bitter. But on ordering a pint I was informed that they only sold Watney's?

"But hold on?" I protested, "It says outside that you sell Tetley's?"

"True," replied the barman, "But if we'd put up a sign saying Watney's, would you have come in?"

You can't argue with logic like that?

Back at the campsite, I glimpsed my first sighting of the mysterious post woman from Sheffield and her suicidal dog, but more about her later. I'm glad to say my ankle was feeling a lot better, but now my right knee had decided to enter into the proceedings and had obviously taken the side of its fellow limb, but they were still out-voted, so onwards we will go tomorrow. Goodnight!

Chapter 8
Gargrave to Horton-in-Ribblesdale

Day 5

Distance 22mls
Total 92mls

The morning when I awoke was misty and overcast but looked promising. After a breakfast of eggs, bacon and spaghetti, washed down with copious amounts of tea and biscuits, I packed my still damp tent and, with a passing nod to the backpacker of the female gender, I headed off in a northerly direction, which was fortunate as that was the same direction as the Pennine Way. I travelled a small B-road out of Gargrave, eventually turning off across fields that led over the gentle slopes of Eshton Moor until I met up with the meandering River Aire. From here to the village of Malham, it would be all low-level scenic walking which, unbeknown to me, was leading me into a false sense of security. But all that later, for now, I was soaking up the atmosphere.

Lush green fields, flowers of every description, a quiet lazy river and a warming sun, I even gained my own heard of cows which started following me across a field, totally ignoring my protestations at not being their owner. I was just glad that the bovine kingdom had never had the inclination to master the art of climbing stiles.

Leaving the nearest thing to a harem that I'll ever have I followed the path which caressed the river through the small sleepy hamlets of Airton and Hanlith, marvelling at the quietude and serenity that can still be found in hidden parts of Britain and pondered how long before some deranged land developer gets his grubby hands on it and bastardises it!

It was along one of these stretches that I spied what could only have been described as a Ninja rabbit? On the other side of the river a solitary member of the Oryctolagus Cuniculus family suddenly bolted across the grass, obviously scared by my presence and, at lightning speed, scaled the vertical face of the dry stone wall where it nestled itself between two vertical top stones, folded it's ears down and, due to its colour, blended in perfectly with the rest of the wall so well that if I hadn't seen it perform this little trick I would never have known it was there? From this point on I proceeded cautiously, checking trees for camouflaged cattle, hedgerows for hidden horses and heather for shrouded sheep!

I reached Malham just as the clouds broke and the rain started, which was fortunate as I had some shopping to do, although this turned out to be a waste of time. In a tourist centre as it is you would expect, especially as there was a campsite down the road, that it would be an easy task to buy a small gas cylinder. Trouble was that most of the shops were shut and those that were open didn't stock them, so I settled for a comb and some postcards instead, which was no substitute. Even the YHA shop was closed, and all this at 10 am on a Wednesday morning! After losing an hour in Malham I pushed on for the central attraction, Malham Cove. It stands in all its splendour about a half mile north of the village, and, at 300ft high, it poses a formidable challenge to all who scale her.

Malham Cove

As I walked down the gravel path that leads to the cove, the rain clouds dispersed and the sun shone down once more as if it was all part of a gigantic stage show put on by mother nature to highlight the huge amphitheatre of rock as you approach. I stood there for some time transfixed by the sheer size of the it, wondering what it must have looked like when the water that flows from Malham Tarn cascaded over the precipice, forming what would have been Britain's highest waterfall, apparently bigger than Niagra, but which now disappears down some sinkholes about a half mile before. After viewing the scene from the bottom looking up, I had to get to the top so I could see it looking down. This meant climbing the very steep steps cut into the stone that ran up the side of the cove and which started with me full of energy and excitement at the wonders to behold, and ended with me completely knackered about half way up and not giving a damn about the bloody views from the top!

Suffice it to say, I did finally reach the top and was treated to some of the finest views so far experienced. I was 300ft above the river floor and 1000ft above sea level looking out onto some of the most beautiful scenery imaginable. And, because of the now crystal clear skies, I could see in every direction of the compass for miles. I couldn't tell you *what* I was looking at because of the limited distance to which my maps extended, but it was exhilarating, to say the least.

Beneath my feet was an extensive area of limestone pavement which was riddled with 'clints', these being gaps in the limestone which have been caused by centuries of erosion and vary in depth and width and which could quite easily lead to a broken leg for any backpacker not taking extra care.

It saddened me to have to leave but time was marching on and I wasn't. So I dragged myself away and on towards Malham Tarn.

While nearing the said tarn I came across an ice-cream van and decided to treat myself, hoping that it wouldn't do too much damage to my expanded waistline. I tried to start up a conversation with the vendor only to be met with a monosyllabic response that went something like;

"Hi ya!" I said with a warm, smiley face.

"Yeah?" he replied with a face that could curdle milk.

"Oh, I'll have a cornet please."

"Right."

He begrudgingly put his paper down then tutted as he retrieved the cones from somewhere beneath the counter. I carried on.

"Busy?"

"Nope."

"Is this a good place for business?"

"Yep."

"Many people come up here this time of year?"

"Nope." etc, etc....

I left him trying to improve his command of the English language by reading the Sun newspaper; I didn't hold out much hope. I was ten yards away from the van when an elderly couple driving an equally elderly Austin Allegro pulled up and asked for directions to Janet's Foss, a picturesque waterfall about a mile from Malham Cove. I now considered myself an expert on Yorkshire, having already walked a fair chunk of it, and poured forth my navigational expertise, pointing them back along the road they'd just come from. They looked puzzled at this and questioned my basis for arriving at that direction of travel? Trying not to show my annoyance at having doubt cast upon my map reading skills, me being a world-weary traveller and all, well, Yorkshire anyway? I proceeded to show them said map confirming my prognosis. With confused looks on their ageing faces and more wrinkles added to already furrowed brows, they turned the car around, thanked me and drove off in search of one waterfall. It wasn't until I had walked about 200yds that I suddenly realised that I wasn't where I thought I was on the map and explained why the elderly couple were confused about my directions, because I had just sent them off heading towards Stainforth, some 5 miles away in totally the wrong direction! Dear Mr & Mrs Allegro, I apologise profusely for the error and blame it on my curdled ice-cream.

I eventually sussed out where I was and continued on the right path for Malham Tarn, which skirted around the beauty spot before coming upon the National Trust Field Studies Centre at Malham Tarn House. Here I was surprised to find a couple of mini-busses parked outside, the sign-writing on their sides stating that they had come up from the town of Hoddesdon, which was only about five miles from my hometown of Harlow. Boy, what a small world!

As a matter of interest, Malham Tarn was the setting for the book, The Water Babies, written by whomever in whenever about whatever? I hope this information has been helpful to you.

Personally, with the tarn and surrounding countryside as it was, I would have preferred to have it as a private house where I could spend countless nights listening to the nocturnal chatter of the wildlife, study the myriad stars shining in the heavens, and watch the water do whatever water does while I enjoyed a glass of burgundy. I made a mental note to write to the National Trust to make them an offer of my rucksack and all its contents for the deeds to the house and would do so as soon as I reached Horton-in-Ribblesdale. I pushed on over the pleasant grassy fields of Malham Moor hoping that the rest of the day would be this easy.

Then it hit me, all 2191ft of it, just standing there glaring at me. Fountains Fell! It wasn't as high Everest, nor as steep as the Matterhorn, just long and arduous with the added infliction of rain and mist thrown in for good measure. Following the path was difficult; there wasn't one. It was just a case of guessing where the top was and heading in that general direction, hoping for the best. As luck would have it I eventually found the summit, but not before having to splash through countless bogs which were three or four feet wide but too long to go round. Fortunately, as I crossed the top to begin the descent, the clouds broke and the sun shone through once more, revealing a good wide path leading down to the road. Unfortunately, the other thing it revealed was the even higher peak of Pen-y-Ghent which, at 2273ft, will be the highest point reached on the walk so far and was thankfully the last climb of the day.

The descent from Fountains Fell was fairly easy, so easy in fact that with my ankle feeling decidedly better I decided to run a little of the way to make up for lost time. This started off as a gentle trot but eventually, what with gravity, momentum and giving a 50lb rucksack a piggyback, turned into a full-scale, headlong, out-of-control career down the mountainside! I finally managed to slow myself down, but by this time the damage to my knee had been done, although I didn't know it at the time. Once down to the road I stopped for a drink of water and a top of Kendal Mint Cake, the mainstay of every earnest walker. Unfortunately, because of its sugary nature, this made me even more thirsty, so I had another drink which in-turn made me hungry, so I had some more mint cake, which made me more thirsty, so....etc, etc.,

The approach to Pen-y-Ghent

I knew what to expect from Pen-y-Ghent having climbed it once before, but I'd forgotten that the last 150ft was a total rock scramble, made even more difficult when carrying a heavy rucksack, and more than a few times I suddenly found myself either starting to fall backwards or slide back down the loose surface. With heart in mouth and lax bowels, I finally made it to the top. The mountain is one of a set of three that make up the Three Peaks way, a famous fell-run which takes in the two other summits of Whernside and Ingleborough, creating a very efficient way of killing yourself.

The village of Horton-in-Ribblesdale was now only three miles distant, reached by a very long track which started off flat and smooth and ended up for the most part stony and full of potholes. This is where my right knee began to question my sanity. Basically, for the last mile, I was doing very good Long John Silver impersonations for the pain in my knee was so bad it became unbearable to walk on. What should have taken me 20mins to complete took me nearly double that?

Finally, I limped into town just gone 6 pm, which is when all the shops and cafes shut, so leaving me with no food for tonight or the morning. 'Oh well,' I thought to myself, 'It looks like I'll have to eat down the pub tonight?' Tut, tut!

After a while I found the campsite, which was no more than a field full of long grass waiting to be flattened by hundreds of campers, thus saving a fortune on petrol for a lawn mower; but in my knackered state, I didn't care. So I pitched up in a nice quiet spot, had a shower in an old stone washroom with one dim light bulb, and ventured down to the local to feast on salad and chips washed down with a couple of pints of local bitter. I daren't have anymore because I was so far away from the toilets; camping I mean, not the pub conveniences? The pub was just how I like them, old, quiet, and serving real ale. What more could I want?

I wandered back to the tent at about 9 and sat worrying about how my leg would hold up tomorrow and if I'd have to abandon the walk after having come so far? But tomorrows a few hours away, so I decided to sleep on it and see what a brand new day would bring.

Chapter 9
Horton-in-Ribblesdale to Hawes

Day 6

Distance 15mls
Total 107mls

What the new day did bring was hunger pains due to lack of breakfast but at least my knee and ankle seemed a lot better, but then again they always do first thing in the morning. With no prospect of being invited to share someone's Wheatabix or even a discarded worm from a passing sparrow, I opted for breaking camp and finding an open shop for a Mars Bar and a pint of milk. The time was 7 am and I spent the next hour walking from one end of the village to the other in the hope of finding a newsagent that in any other normal town would be open from 6 am till 10 pm. But here, in sleepy Horton-in-Ribblesdale, there was no chance of even finding the milkman up before noon! So I added another hole to my belt and tightened up so as to stifle the pitiful cries of hunger emanating from my stomach which had been expecting some form of nourishment before heading off for another days trudging.

The path followed a gravel and stone track which, if you avoided the larger stones, was easy going underfoot, but if you didn't was extremely painful. The track itself, or Harber Scar Lane to give it its full title, gradually increased in elevation as it followed the contours or Horton Moor, passing a series of deep potholes and caves along the way. The first of these is Sell Gill Holes; a small gaping chasm into which tumbles the water that runs down from the moor and which, if you stand too close, gives you the feeling that if you're not careful it won't be the only thing tumbling into the pothole. Next, passed in quick succession, is Jackdaw Hole, Cowskull Pot (70ft deep), Pen-y-Ghent Long Churn (180ft) and Canal Cavern. After this fascinating array of holes and chasms, the path finally leaves the track and cuts down a short distance across fields to pass Old Ing Farm, a lonely dwelling that affords vivid views of Ingleborough across the valley. That's on fine days that is, and today had just stopped being a fine day. That old backpacker's friend (or should I say fiend), mist, had reared its ugly head again, except this time visibility was down to about 30yds and stayed that way until I reached Hawes. Not only that, but it started raining as well just to rub salt into the wound.

Jackdaw Hole

After about 12 miles of damp, sodden, miserably boring trudge, I was beginning to get fed up and lose heart when I heard the sound that every walker hopes he'll never hear; six blasts on a whistle indicating somebody's in trouble; maybe lost, possibly injured? "Bugger!" I said to myself, panic setting in "This may be where I'll have to put my first aid skills into operation? How will I cope? What should I do first? Will I do the right thing?"

Then I began to think perhaps I was wrong. Maybe it was someone down in the valley training sheepdogs, or perhaps there was a whistle factory nearby and somebody was testing them? Oh well, I won't know until I get there so let's keep going and hope for the best.

Eventually, I came across the 'emergency'. Four elderly walkers had become separated along the path and decided to keep blowing their whistles until they caught up with each other! I didn't know whether to shake their hands in relief or wring their necks in anger! Inconsiderate acts like this cost time and money to the Mountain Rescue teams who are already stretched to the limit. I walked away thinking to myself that people like them should not be allowed out alone and wishing that I could have thought of the right words to say to make my annoyance felt, but instead I opted for putting as much distance between me and them as possible.

Bridge over Ling Gill

After this little burst of unwanted excitement, the path started its descent down towards Hawes, and this is where my problems started. Up to now, I hadn't had a whimper from my right leg, but once I started the downward journey all hell broke loose. The trouble this time was my upper thigh muscle, or quadriceps to give it its proper anatomical title. Every time I took a step with my right leg I received an agonising shooting pain through the muscle. I tried everything to cure the problem, even so far as to removing my trousers and applying half a pound of Deep Heat and a full-length elasticated bandage – but to no avail. Eventually, I settled for the only course of action left open to me, the 'Macho March!' This consisted of me swearing loudly at my right leg every time I took a step in the hope of masking the pain and went something like;

Left
Right..."Come on you bastard!"
Left
Right..."You won't beat me!"
Left
Right..."Is that the best you can do??"
Left
Right..."C'mon you cow-son!"
Left
Right..."Go on, give it your best shot!"

And so on and so on till I reached Hawes. Rather unconventional, but it did the trick.

Once the market town and level ground were reached the problem ceased, so the answer lay in finding flat hills and level mountains from now on.

I entered Hawes through a back passage, (no *double entente* meant but probably taken), which brings you out onto the main high street. Immediately turning left I made straight for a café at the top end of the town which I knew about from a previous stay some 12 years before. On that occasion, my wife and I were camped at a site just on the outskirts of the town but close enough for nightly visits to the local watering holes. One event that will always stick in my wife's mind was a midday saunter into the town for provisions, followed by a pint or three at my insistence. At the time she was suffering badly from a stiff neck and when we got back to the tent I offered to massage it for her. All went well until I decided to do what I'd seen all good doctors do on TV for people with stiff necks; wait until the patient is completely relaxed and then give it a quick twist, thus curing the problem. Unfortunately, her problem was nothing to do with the joints, it was purely muscular. The scream could be heard all over the campsite and brought people rushing from their tents to see who was being murdered while I, in my semi-alcoholic stupor, was trying in vain to clamp my hand over her mouth to stifle the wailing while at the same time becoming entangled in the bedroom compartment which seemed to have moved from its original position in the melee. Her expletives are unprintable here, and her neck has never been the same since.

After a nourishing, wholesome, healthy meal of double egg and chips followed by fruitcake, I decided on some shopping to replenish dwindling stocks, namely Kendal Mint Cake. On leaving one of the shops I was accosted by none other than the lady postman and her four-legged friend who asked if they could walk with me to the campsite (the girl, not the dog), which just happened to be the same site I stayed at before. We travelled to the other end of the town chatting about this and that but with frequent interruptions from her enquiring if we were going in the right direction. That's the second time in two days my navigational expertise was being brought into question. The audacity of these amateurs! I assured her that the campsite we were heading for was the very same one I'd stayed at previously and knew exactly where it was, pointing out that the map must be wrong. Imagine my surprise when turning the corner of the lane which leads up to the site, to find a totally empty field? Not a tent to be seen anywhere? Not even a standpipe? The look on her face said it all.

"Where the hell's it gone?" I said standing there dumbfounded.

"It's probably where it says it is on the map?" she replied.

"But it should be here, it *was* here?" I protested.

"Well not according to the map?" she retorted.

"They must have moved it?" was the only thing I could think to say.

Unfortunately, I was saying it to myself for she was already halfway down the lane, following her map. She put forward the suggestion that maybe it was a different site, but this I dismissed due to the fact that it was run by the same people it was 12 years ago whose name I'll never forget because they sounded as if they were straight out of a Monty Python sketch; Mr & Mrs Dinsdale. If you're reading this, Mr & Mrs Dinsdale, please write and tell me I'm not going mad??

We finally made it to the site at around 4 pm with the sun now glowing warm and the air still. I set about pitching my tent after being unable to find anybody to book with and was told by other campers to 'sort it out in the morning'. I couldn't believe my eyes when my companion started to pitch up to her tent because it was a cheap, heavy, two-man affair with cumbersome poles and a weighty canvas flysheet. This explained why she told me she had to stop every hour for a rest. Add to this the fact that she carried tins of dog food, thick woollen jumpers and umpteen maps and books, along with all her other belongings, all stuffed into an old heavy canvas, exterior framed rucksack. She was a disaster waiting to happen.

After showering I decided to take advantage of their washing machine and tumble dryer and do my smalls, which seemed a good idea at the time but which eventually took me nearly three hours due to the inefficiency of the drier. As I'd decided to wash just about everything it was no surprise to find me sitting on the drier in my underpants when Miss Tarzan walked in. But, as is with all backpackers it's an accepted thing, so no one takes any notice, which is a polite way of saying she didn't take any notice of me. I left her doing her undies and retired to bed happy in the knowledge that, if nothing else, at least I'll be wearing clean pants tomorrow, which would please my mum. The other pleasing thought was that tomorrow night would see me supping real ale and experiencing real music at the Tan Hill Inn, something I'd been looking forward to ever since starting the Way. I went to sleep a contented walker.

Chapter 10
Hawes to Tan Hill Inn

Day 7

Distance 17mls
Total 124mls

Leaving Hawes

I left Hawes early this morning for two reasons. Firstly, so as I didn't end up being hitched up with our female walker and her dog; and secondly, so as I didn't have to pay for the nights camp as the shop didn't open till 9 am, tight little backpacker that I am. About 1½mls out of Hawes I came to the small hamlet of Hardrow where I was tempted to visit the spectacular waterfall of Hardrow Force. This is the highest waterfall in the country, cascading some 96ft in a single drop into a ravine of rock and which, because of its overhanging lip and erosion at its base, enables you to walk behind the fall. The reason for passing up the opportunity is because, not only had I seen it before, but to gain entrance to the gorge you have to pass through the Green Dragon Inn, paying a small fee to do so, and at this time of the morning no one was around. After leaving the farm track that the PW follows out of Hardrow I was faced with the next challenge, the summit of Great Shunner Fell. To reach the top entailed a long, laborious, boggy, five-mile trudge, only made easier by the far-ranging views of the distant surrounding hills. It was about two hours later that the summit was conquered and was celebrated in true British fashion with a cup of tea. I sat with my back against the ordnance survey trig point looking west across to the distant peaks of the Lake District, promising myself that if ever I could afford to I'd be living there one day. But for now, all I could do was look and dream.

A brisk breeze was blowing across the peak and as a result, I became chilled quite quickly, which was reason enough to get off my bum and proceed with the walk, although I felt sad to leave Cumbria, even though it was 40mls or so away. The descent was just as bad as the ascent, being boggy and arduous, and only made easier by the meeting with a middle-aged couple who told me that I would soon come across a farm track that complete the last 1½mls of the walk from Great Shunner Fell down into Thwaite.

As predicted the track was soon reached, not only the track but also an American couple who enquired as to how far it was to the summit. I was totally gob-smacked! Here we were on one of the most exposed and desolate mountains around, (Great Shunner Fell being 2340ft high), and here they were attired as if going out for a round of golf! Him; dressed in a thin nylon sports jacket, open-necked shirt, check trousers and flat, white leather shoes; She, in an identical jacket, blouse, slacks and high heeled shoes. I asked if they were serious about trying to reach the top dressed like that, and they looked at me as if there was a problem.
"Why?" said Mr American, "Is it bad up there?"
"Not dressed like me, but certainly like you?" I replied. "If you go up there like that you'll definitely be a Mountain Rescue job!"
"Oh, in that case, we better just walk to the end of the lane and come back again, Harry." His wife interjected as she struggled to stop her heels sinking into the farm track.
"Thanks!" said Mrs American, "Have a nice day!"
"Yeesss!" I replied, a slight hint of sarcasm in my voice.

I left them tippy-toeing between the puddles and cowpats; her with handbag, him with video camera, unaware of the dangers of exposure in a place like this. I'm sure they thought that I, wearing stout leather walking boots, thick cords, a body warmer, cagoule and a woollen hat and gloves was just part of the quaint local dress in these parts.

Summit of Great Shunner Fell

As if on a well-rehearsed cue, the sun, which had been playing coy all morning, now shone down to illuminate my emergence into the beautiful village of Thwaite, creating a scene that looked straight out of a picture postcard. Thwaite is reminiscent of those pretty English villages shown in films portraying the turn-of-the-century life and up to now has stayed largely unspoiled, with a tea room and a B&B being the only lean of tourism visible. Unfortunately, the walk doesn't stay long in the village unless you wander back and forth for a couple of hours just to soak in the atmosphere and peacefulness, which I would have done had it not been for the beer pumps of Tan Hill Inn now only seven miles away calling to me.

For those of less resolve, it seems easier to turn left in the village and follow the B6270 straight to Keld, which was only 1½mls away. But true devotees of the Pennine Way will stick to the official route and traverse Kisdon Hill, taking the long way round. Those that do will be rewarded with some spectacular views of the River Swale flowing down through the dale of the same name for the path follows a contour line of around 1600ft which overlooks the valley and gives elevated views of the river. I passed a farmhouse situated high up on Kisdon and, realising that my water supply was low, was going to stop and ask for a refill, but being one unable to placate vicious guard dogs with an unconvincing "Sit boy, nice doggy," I opted instead to fill my bottle from an old pipe that was sticking out of a wall pouring peaty coloured water into a tin bath. I made sure I added a couple of Puritabs in the hope of killing anything, not of this planet that may now be practising backstroke in my water bottle.

River Swale from Kidson Hill

The ability to admire the views was hampered by the fact that every step had to be carefully placed due to the uneven surface and large rocks strewn about the place, but every hundred yards or so was a good excuse to stop and rest and drink in the scenery. Two miles further on Kisdon Force is reached; a small but impressive waterfall nestled in a wooded ravine and a pleasant place for a cup of tea. Although not actually on the PW, it's worth the detour. Pushing on over Stonesdale Moor the landscape becomes flat and dull, a letdown from the rest of the day's walk but at least now the pub was in site, which was incentive enough to perk up and finish the day.

Four miles later saw me standing in its car park. The one thing other than the walk itself that had kept me going and the one place that I wanted to be able to say I'd visited, the TAN HILL INN. At 1785ft above sea level, it's the highest pub in Britain, and probably the most desolate into the bargain. At the time it was famous not only because of its geographical situation but also because of the adverts made years ago by Ted Moult, advertising Everest Double Glazing windows. There were two amusing facts about this. The first being that in the advert, Ted extols the virtues of the windows saying how air-tight and soundproof they were, and then proceeds to tell his associate, who's standing outside, to "Switch the fan on, 'arry!" which Harry duly does, thus destroying the validity of the windows being soundproof. The second fact being that planning permission hadn't actually been granted for the windows, so they all had to be removed, not gaining permission until much later on when the windows could be replaced again.

I pitched up on the open moorland which surrounds the pub in record time and headed straight for the bar for an evening of real ale, Yorkshire fare and traditional music played by local musicians on authentic instruments, just like on the 'Go With Noakes!' TV programme where I first saw it. Imagine my disgust to be confronted by gassy beer, a blaring jukebox and two inebriated farmers who insisted on me joining them at the bar for a drink. Even sitting at a far table didn't discourage them for one farmer came over, picked up my pint, and took it back to the bar so I'd have to follow him and consequently sit there and talk to them, which was probably impossible to do when they were sober because of their broad Yorkshire accent, let alone when they were half cut, or in their case, full cut! As for the Yorkshire fare, I settled in the end for an omelette while the two drunken sots stuffed their faces with ham and chips which they then proceeded to share with the rest of the pub when they started trying to sing Irish ballads, thus spraying the rest of the customers with half-chewed helpings of food. I finally managed to slip away to another bar when one of them went to the toilet and the other started helping himself to another pint while the landlady was out the back. She herself looked like she could have taken on half the pub in a twelve round fight, with a five-gallon barrel of beer under each arm just to give the others a chance, and still win hands down.

I settled in front of a glowing log fire, safe in the knowledge that the table was too far away from the beer pumps for the farmers to venture. And so I finally relaxed and enjoyed what was left of a dream-ruined evening. About ten minutes later I was joined by the female postie and a depressed looking dog who slumped himself down in front of the hearth and refused to budge for the rest of the evening. I tried striking up a conversation with her but this proved extremely hard work and became reminiscent of the monologue I had with the ice-cream vendor at Malham. So instead I bought her a coffee and we just sat there letting the fire entertain us. Not long after that, we were joined by four other 'Wayers' who I'd run across a couple of times along the walk but not really spoken to. Actually, three of them were doing the PW from YHA to YHA, and the other was doing Wainwrights very own Coast-to-Coast walk and had agreed to meet at Keld where the two paths crossed. Soon after they sat with us she and her canine companion departed for their tent for the night. Immediately this happened the conversation turned to talking about her and how she'd managed to walk this far with all that weight, and how ill-prepared she'd been never having attempted a walk of this calibre. As a matter of fact, the one thing I did glean from her was that the only real walking experience she had was between letterboxes in downtown Sheffield. We also came to the conclusion that the dog was now looking decidedly depressed and probably suicidal and was just waiting for the right moment when he could either push her over a cliff or jump himself? I told them how first thing in the morning he would be leaping and jumping all over the place like a new puppy, obviously thinking she'd finally come to her senses and was going home, and then quickly reverting back to a mood of despair when he realised she wasn't. The only thing I wasn't able to tell them about her was her name as I'd never thought to ask it or offer mine in that case, and never got round to it all the times I met her, hence the reason for the descriptive titles for her. But from now on, to make things easier and because I'm running out of adjectives, I'll refer to her as Doris, because she looked like a Doris.

Kidson Force

The evening turned out to be quite enjoyable in the end, due more to the company than the surroundings, so-much-so that I ended up having three pints of bitter and about five shots of Port. I finally bid my drinking companions goodnight and fell into my tent about 11 pm thinking I was probably going to regret it in the morning, but for now, I fell asleep a happy man.

Chapter 11
Tan Hill Inn to Middleton in Teesdale

Day8

Distance 17mls
Total 141mls

Alas, another day started without breakfast due to it slipping my mind to buy provisions last night for some reason. I was surprised to find that my head was totally clear this morning, much to my relief, so with no point in delaying any further, I left before Doris broke camp. I wouldn't have been averse to walking with her but her pace would be slow, the conversation laboured and me, being the consummate gentleman (I know because my mum told me), would have felt sorry for her and offered to lighten her load to make it easier for her. This probably would have resulted in me first carrying her maps, then her books, followed by her food, clothes, sleeping bag, tent and probably the dog as well; so best I trundle on alone.

The next six miles were of boggy, gentle sloping, absolutely boring walking, interspersed with exciting moments where I would find the elusive path hidden amongst the endless peat groughs. No change there. And, just in case Doris had left and was thinking about trying to catch up with me, I quickened my pace, nearly breaking into a run.

The Way for the most part follows first Frumming Beck and then Sleightholme Beck before reaching Trout Heads Farm where you're given a choice of routes, either staying on the official path or diverting down to the town of Bowes, which adds four miles to the journey. I pondered on whether to take the alternative route knowing there would be refreshments and a chance to re-stock my provisions but opted in the end for a shorter walk and a tighter belt. About a mile further on I came across Gods Bridge, a natural limestone arch that spans the River Greta. I half expected it to be manned by archangels (security), angels (toll officers), Seraphim (traffic wardens) and harp playing cherubs (muzak), easing the journey across. How disappointing to find just a grass-covered piece of flat rock about 8ft long? But then again, a celestial span manned by a heavenly host in the middle of a moor may have looked somewhat out of place, even for County Durham. And, try as I might, I couldn't see Him anywhere? Perhaps he was submerged up to his waist in some glutinous morass somewhere? Being omnipotent and almighty was one thing: walking on peat bogs was something else.

The barren Sleightholm Moor

Next obstacle was the dreaded A66, which proved more difficult to cross than Kinder Scout. The only thing that tried to run me down up there was an irate pheasant who I just managed to evade at the last second when it came tearing straight out of the heather about 10ft from me and aimed directly for my head. But here, being weighed down by half a camping shop in my rucksack and most of northern England on my boots; even a Robin Reliant at a distance of two miles against a 90mph headwind had a fair chance of hitting me before I could make the other side. Suffice it to say I did make it and decided to knock at a cottage situated by the road for a water refill before carrying on. A middle-aged gentleman answered the door and, eyeing me very suspiciously, took my bottle, closing the door in my face as he did so. I wondered if he thought it was a gift and that would be the last I saw of him, or my water. I shouldn't have worried though for he was back at his door less than ten seconds later, thrusting the bottle in my hand and closing the door in my face mid-thank-you, again without uttering a single word. I didn't look that frightening, did I?

The route from here to Blackton Reservoir was easy and uninspiring, the only thing of interest being four groups of soldiers out on manoeuvres who passed me going in the other direction and, even though they were weighed down with equipment that made my rucksack look like a 'Jiffy bag', they were actually 'yomping' it, in other words they were jogging along as if they were carrying a bag of feathers on their backs.

By the time I reached Blackton Reservoir my stomach had convinced itself my throat had been cut, and, with no hope of coming across civilisation soon, I decided to break into my survival rations and cooked myself up a bowl of soup. I did this while sitting next to the water channel that feeds the lower reservoir from the higher one, or should have except that water levels were so low that there was only a trickle running between them. A very worrying site indeed.

With only six miles to go I could have skipped lunch and waited till I reached the campsite, but I was making good time and decided to rest for an hour or so while I took in the peace and solitude that was all around me but which I hadn't really noticed because most of the time I was too wrapped up in getting my head down and getting stuck into completing the day.

The silence was deafening and the scenery blinding and I was sad in the fact I could only afford to spend two weeks on the Pennine Way for so much was missed when working to a tight schedule. I know I could have walked it in sections, but the challenge for me was to walk it in one go while carrying everything on my back and roughing it each night. Originally I had planned not to use sites but just to camp where and when I felt like it but was told that this is not allowed in any of the National Parks along the way unless it was an emergency, and it would have been difficult trying to explain every night's camp as an emergency for they would have probably revoked my backpackers union card, tore up my O.S. maps and publicly burnt my walking boots, threatening me with immediate deportation if I was ever found rambling again.

It took a lot of convincing on the part of my legs before they would respond and get up off their backside, but this they did after I promised them an easy days walking tomorrow. I suppose a hint of celebration could be had at this point because according to Wainwright, I was at the exact halfway stage of the walk, 135mls completed with only another 135mls to go. But my Footprint maps only gave it as being 128mls, so somebody somewhere was telling porkies? But in the interest of getting my body to complete the walk, I opted for Wainwrights' estimations, considering he'd actually walked the damn thing! And not only that, but his calculations seemed seven miles closer to the way my body felt?

The walk to Harter Fell was simple enough, but due to insufficient detail on the map, I became, in backpackers speak, misguided; or in layman's terms, lost? This was only a temporary delay and I finally found the correct path over the hill. Once there I was treated to stunning views of Teesdale, laid out before me like an unfolded map with all the details coloured in. "There," I said to my legs, "See what I told you, a nice days walk tomorrow!" They didn't answer but kept on moving ever onward and downward. Just over the brow of the hill I chanced upon an old boy rebuilding a dry-stone wall and got chatting to him. This proved to be another mistake, not because of unfriendliness but because he was so difficult to understand, what with his broad northern accent and me with my narrow southern ears. I finally gathered that he used to work for the farmer and bought this field off him for his own use but which meant that he would have to do all the repairs himself, which included an old barn as well as the walls. The subject somehow got round to pubs and he told me that he used to drink in the Tan Hill Inn until they brought in the juke-boxes and pool tables, and that was enough for him. In this, I could sympathise a great deal and left him feeling some sought of a common bond between us. But that could have been the sheep droppings I'd stepped in.

Middleton-in-Teesdale from Harter Fell

I hadn't gone more than 20yds from the old man when who should appear but Doris and Fido. Where the hell did they come from? Seeing as how there was only a mile to go to Middleton-in-

Teesdale we walked together, me all the time trying to find out which bus she had caught as she had already confided in me that the day before she hadn't walked over Kisdon Hill to Keld, but walked up the B6270 instead and then kept on the road until she got to the Tan Hill Inn, which explains why she wasn't that far behind me?

We arrived at the site at the end of a warm sunny day, both hungry and thirsty and in need of a shower and rest, separately of course! I made straight for the camp shop and bought a tin of mince, a tin of new potatoes and a tin of rice pudding, plus a packet or two of biscuits. Any other time I would have turned my nose up at such scant fare, but this evening it was a feast fit for a king and I partook gladly. Suitably replenished, I headed straight for the showers where I got talking to a couple of athletic looking walkers who were doing it north to south, eventually asking each other obvious question, "What's it like further on?" I told them all I could, which consisted mainly of bogs, bogs and more bogs broken up by countless peat groughs, and was greeted by the same news, which basically sums up most of the Pennine Way in one noun. They told me that tomorrows walk was probably one of the best days walking on the whole route, but that the day after was a real killer. This I didn't want to hear, thinking that the walk over Fountains Fell and Pen-y-Ghent in one go was the worst day experienced so far. Obviously, I was going to be proved wrong?

I had intended to do some washing but the facilities looked a bit knackered so, not wanting to risk having a rucksack full of wet clothes again, I opted for leaving them and having a drink in the bar instead. Once again I met the other two hikers and sat down to share a pint with them. As usual most of the evening was spent talking about the Way, it's good points and bad points, bits to watch out for, bits to avoid, all-in-all most of the talk seemed to be centred around the bad bits. Talk eventually turned to occupations, mine being office partitioning and suspended ceilings, which I thought might be quite interesting to some people, until I discovered that they were both prison officers, one of them being the P.T. instructor, hence the reason for their level of fitness and also hence the reason they were aiming to do between 30 to 40mls a day, bless them. Thing was, they were achieving it! Having an interest in martial arts, I was curious as to what sort of restraining techniques they used on prisoners and was told they basically used anything they could for with a lot of prisoners it was a case of going in mob-handed as one or two officers on their own wouldn't be able to handle the situation, especially when an inmate was intent on doing as much damage as possible to the staff. Apparently, one of the favourite tricks is the eye gouge punch where, as they punch an officer in the face, they would stick their thumb in the eye socket and pop it out. With these sorts of tactics being used what chance do you stand? Obviously, they were restricted as to what they could tell me but what little they did was very interesting and useful to my ends and made for a pleasant evenings chat, although probably not everybody's cup of tea.

As with other encounters we finished that night wishing each other good luck and hoped we might see each other again in years to come, trying for a second or third attempt.

Chapter 12
Middleton-in-Teesdale to Dufton

Day 9

Distance 21mls
Total 162mls

I awoke today to decide upon a problem that reared its ugly head last night; should I, shouldn't I? Today was originally was going to be a day of rest as it was the midway point of the walk and I was on schedule, but then I decided I'd rather get the walk over and done with as soon as possible and get home for early a couple of days R&R before the slog of work had to be faced again. Problem was that before I went to sleep last night I noticed my right calf muscle had swollen up quite badly and my ankle, in a display of solidarity with its walking partner, had broken out in sympathy. In the morning light, they looked decidedly better, although not perfect. Today's walking, if the two Olympic marathon walkers from last night were to be believed, should be a lot easier on the feet, so perhaps it may not pose a problem, or it could make things worse? What to do? My ego made the decision for me, for as I emerged from my cosy little cocoon I noticed Doris hurriedly stuffing her tent and equipment into her rucksack, obviously determined to be first away this morning. 'So?' I thought to myself, 'The gauntlet has been thrown down?' How would it have looked to my occasional walking companions had the over-burdened slip of a thing dragged herself into Dufton at the end of the day exhausted but triumphal whilst I, the hunter-gatherer, the slayer of wild beasts and protector of nations was laid up in my tent because I had a boo-boo?

I finally left the campsite about half hour after her and trundled down to the River Tees where the P.W. closely follows its course for about 11mls. What was disturbing was a gathering of a number of mountain rescue vehicles and volunteer ambulances that had assembled at the start of the walk and I began to wonder if maybe this section wasn't as easy as my two drinking companions had led me to believe and that perhaps today was going to be my Swansong? With lump in throat, I girded my loins (ouch!) and pushed on to see what the day held in store. I eventually sussed that there was some sort of exercise going on as regards the rescue teams, which was also coupled with a half-marathon run alongside the river. Throw in a backpacker or ten and you've got what amounts to a pretty hectic Sunday morning along what is normally a quite sedate River Tees.

River Tees

Fortunately, whatever was going on was kept away from the path itself, which left a very pleasant walk through bluebell-laden fields and quiet strolls by the riverbanks. After three or four miles Wynch Bridge footbridge was reached which only offered access for those of stout heart due to the fact that a sign posted on the bridge warned the crossee against any sort of extreme usage which might include 'jumping, swinging, running, hopping, dancing, tumbling, somersaulting, skateboarding, pole-vaulting or any other 'ing' that may cause the bridge to collapse. This also included more than one person using the bridge at any one time, probably piggybacking? Excellent views of Low Force, a small waterfall, were obtained from the bridge but it has nothing on its big brother further up the river.

Navigation here was totally unnecessary as the path was so well defined that you could follow it blindfolded at night, so it gave you the opportunity to take in all that was around you without having to refer back to the map or compass every five minutes. As High Force is approached the path follows a gravel track which has been specially laid between differing bushes, shrubs and plants to give one the feeling of walking in a garden. Not being a gardener, I couldn't tell you what kind of bushes, shrubs and plants they were but they aided to mask the view of the waterfall, leaving only the roaring sound of the tumult which increases in volume as you near it until you suddenly emerge at a viewpoint which overlooks the spectacle, taking your breath away with both its ferocity and beauty. This wasn't enough for me, so I quickly made my way to the waterfall itself where you can stand virtually on top and look down into the tumbling, thundering wall of water cascading 70ft into the chasm below where it almost instantly reverts back to a gentle rolling river as if nothing has happened. It was also here that I nearly fell over Doris and Rover taking snapshots of the waterfall, (Doris, not the dog), both looking decidedly tired already. So I grabbed the chance and quickly buggered off before she recovered her composure and joined me!

The easiness of the path never really abated, even when the short, steep slopes of High Crag were reached. Here, on the brow of the hill, was found a large tent which housed a brood of time checkers waiting for the arrival of who knows what. On my emergence onto the hill they suddenly spotted me and, like a swarm of bees that had just seen an open honeypot, homed in on me for the kill. Because of their eagerness to time, label, position and quantify me, it wasn't until they were practically upon me that they suddenly realised what I was and dragged themselves back to their tent dejectedly, only stopping to offer a brief "Sorry, we thought you were one of the marathon runners?" as a half-hearted apology for scaring the daylights out of me. I left the hill glad that I wasn't fit enough to be a runner and safe in the knowledge that at the end of the P.W. at least I won't be beaten to a pulp by a gaggle of timekeepers.

Ever onward I pushed, accompanied by the relaxing swirling and lapping of the Tees as it makes its way down toward the North Sea and freedom.

On reaching Falcon Clints, the first real challenge of the day was met. Here, between the river bank and the sharp rise of the hill face, was a mass, no, a mess of boulders and rocks which had to be navigated over as there was no possible way around them. This slowed the proceedings down to almost a complete stop for the rocks were slippery from mosses and lichens growing on them and a sure bet for a broken leg if not careful.

Cauldron Snout

Like High Force, I heard Cauldron Snout long before I ever saw it, and when I did finally see it, I couldn't believe it? Here before me was one of the most powerful waterfalls I had ever seen! It even put High Force to shame in its ferociousness. I stopped for a cup of tea and endless photos and wished that I could camp here for the night so I could fall asleep listening to the anger and bellowing of its raging waters as they plunge 200ft over the rocks which break the fall turning them into a series of falls, otherwise it would be the highest fall in Britain. Unfortunately, I couldn't camp there or even stop there any longer for the day was getting shorter and so were my energy reserves.

So, on over Rasp Hill I ventured, ever aware of the fact that just to my left was an MoD artillery range, and, to make them aware of this insignificant walker, I donned my bright orange cagoule, which then got me wondering about whether the targets they used were orange and if so was I setting myself up as a moving target? I spent most of the next two miles walking sideways with my back to the range in the hope that if they were using small rounds then perhaps my rucksack would stop them, and, if it were anything bigger, then I wouldn't feel it anyway! Fortunately, either they weren't playing today or they were pretty lousy shots, either way, I made High Cup in one piece.

High Cup comes up on you suddenly and without warning due to the fact that the ground slopes gently up to the edge, thus not really exposing itself until you reach the lip of this awesome spectacle. And what a breathtaking spectacle it is! This geological wonder stops you dead in your tracks, which is rather fortunate otherwise you'd plummet some 600ft to the valley floor below where the views of the Lake District aren't as good.

High Cup

It is the result of glacial erosion and as a consequence, the sides sweep smoothly down to the valley floor leaving the rim practically dead level all the way around with the open end facing SW towards Cumbria. As I stood there mouth agape, the clouds broke and the sun unveiled itself as if on cue to highlight the valley and the mountains beyond. This combined with the myriad hues of green and brown, the ambient tranquillity and the overwhelming feeling of contentedness was pure

Nirvana. Had I died at that moment it couldn't have been a more beautiful setting.

While I stood there drinking in the awesome phenomenon before me, another walker along with his dog joined me and we got chatting about the equanimity of the scene and what it would be like to live here. We stood for what felt like an eternity, both of us lost in our imaginations and dreams, but time was swiftly passing and there was still four miles to go before camp, so together we walked all the way down to Dufton, the end of today's jaunt, with me having to stop frequently due to the fact that my leg muscle was playing up again. But, seeing as how it was a lovely sunny afternoon, neither of us wanted to rush things anyway.

It came out in conversation that he was originally from Chelmsford, which is about 30mins from my hometown, but was now living in the Lake District while being in charge of an Outward Bound/Management Stress centre. This now gave me two reasons to hate him! First, because I want to live in the Lake District; and second, because I've always wanted to be involved in an Outward Bound or Survival school and, seeing as I had more chance of winning the football pools, it would seem both are just a dream. Having said that, at the time I was in the throes of trying to set up a company with some associates staging adventure weekends in Essex which would be a sort of testing ground for those wishing to attempt an Outward Bound course but were put off by the amount of travelling involved, as most schools were either in Scotland, Wales, Cumbria or Yorkshire, with a few down in the West Country. Unfortunately, due to one thing and another and a lack of commitment from other people, the idea was dropped and forgotten about.

I reached Dufton hot, sweaty and in pain, but all the happier for the chance to gaze upon three of the most beautiful sights in this part of the country, and all in one day to boot! My companion and I shook hands and I thanked him for the company and his help in taking my mind off my leg.

The campsite was nothing more than a large field overrun with sheep and lambs who, for some strange reason, found it necessary to keep trying to eat my guy ropes. After shooing them away for the umpteenth time I decided to limp down to the YHA to purchase some provisions as the only shop in Dufton closes at 5 pm and it was already 5.01. The main street of Dufton is not what is normally thought of as a main street as found in most towns. It's more of a wide lane, edged with green grassed expanses and shaded with mature trees, in itself surrounded by old cottages and period houses in a village where, if a coach and horses were driven up the main street, no one would bat an eyelid. As a matter of fact, to see a car driven through village makes you feel like you're in some sought of time warp.

As I approached the door of the hostel I noticed a very sad if not depressed looking dog sitting outside. No? It can't be? Yep! On entering, there she stood; still wearing the thick woollen jumper she had started out with this morning even though the temperature was now close to 20c! She was trying to buy some dog food, which they obviously didn't stock, but instead let her have half a tin of cat food that the hostel pussy was due to get but which was probably going to have to go on a nocturnal scavenge for tonight's dinner instead. Lucky for me she was staying on another site down the road. So I ambled back to my tent safe in the knowledge that I wouldn't have to compete for a quick getaway in the morning. I arrived back at my canvas and nylon abode where I was met by the presence of another tent quite close to mine? It always amazes me that it doesn't matter where you camp in a field, there's always somebody who has to camp right next to you, even though the rest of the site is empty! On this occasion, though the chap turned out to be quite pleasant and was himself doing the Way, and like me, preferred to keep himself to himself.

For the rest of the evening, I was kept amused watching the lambs gambolling and frolicking and was amazed just how much like children they were. They would all stand in one group seemingly minding their own business and suddenly one would make a mad dash for the other side of the field, which would signal the others to do likewise, and they would all run frantically after him. Then, when they'd reached the other side, they would stop and stand there for a few moments, then another lamb would suddenly run back to where they had started from, followed by the rest of the pack. This went on for around half an hour until the farmer moved them on, probably thinking that the campers had been entertained long enough. I spent the rest of the remaining daylight gazing at one of tomorrow's objectives, Knock Fell, with the highest point on the walk also being reached as well, that of Cross Fell at 2930ft, and all of it in an upward direction.

I was not looking forward to tomorrows walk – and nor was my leg?

Chapter 13
Dufton to Alston

Day 10

Distance 21mls
Total 183mls

I should really have left Dufton a lot earlier considering the amount of distance to be covered, but I didn't get away until 7 am which meant a lot of ground to be made up, either before Cross Fell or afterwards if I was to make Alston before closing time.

I left Dufton under an already blazing sun, which, if this was an indication of the day's weather, then today was going to be one hard, hot slog! The path followed the road out of the village and then turned off up a farm track, eventually making its way over a field thick with dew-laden grass and covered with the prints of early morning wildlife that had now returned to nests and burrows, aware that this time of the day is dangerous and full of hazards, particularly those of the human kind. After a short while, the path picked up another farm track that climbed steadily around Dufton Pike and Browber Hill before turning off over Swindale Beck to carry on its journey up to Knock Fell. Just the other side of the beck the path turns sharp right, and so should have I, but, because I had my head down, I missed the turning and walked a further 300yds before realising. I doubled back and found the right path but then wished I hadn't because, just like the mountain, it went straight up! I found myself having to stop every 100ft or so to take a breather, due in part to a heavy load, hot weather and being overweight, to say nothing of being unfit? Basically, all the prerequisites for a heart attack.

I eventually came upon the three cairns that signify that the summit of Knock Fell had been reached and wondered why the views were so stinted. It was only after a few minutes that I realised that these were the lower cairns and that I had another 800ft to go before reaching the summit proper! So, eight rest periods later saw me, in fact, emerge onto the top of Knock Fell, all 2604ft of it, and yes, the views were much, much better. By this time the weather alternated between being unbearably hot and bearably overcast and saw me doing multiple changes of attire from body warmer to T-shirt and back to body warmer, which was eventually left on due to the exposure of the winds on the summit. Looking north, the next objective of 2780ft Great Dun Fell all but 1¼ miles away, stared at me as if to say "Well, that's the first one done, can you make the second?" "Bloody right I can!" I thought to myself.

Surprisingly enough I'd felt nothing from my leg or my ankle up to now and started to think that whatever it was had finally been beaten. I spoke too soon. Just as I began the descent of the peak it started acting up again. This forced me to follow the tarmac road which leads to the telecommunications centre perched on Great Dun Fell and helped walking enormously, making things a damn sight easier on my leg.

Communications center, Great Dun Fell

The peak was reached and crossed, which meant cutting through the boundary of the telecom centre, a hideous indictment of the total disregard by the authorities of anything scenic, natural and beautiful. How anybody could cold-bloodedly mar such a glorious piece of landscape is beyond me. I suppose we should all be thankful that they only picked on the one peak; they could have desecrated them all?

Little Dun Fell at 2761ft was only just dwarfed by its big brother by 19ft, but this made no real difference as regards climbing it. It certainly didn't feel 19ft shorter? At this point it started to resemble a roller-coaster ride, having dropped 104ft from Knock Fell, then climbing 280ft to Great Dun Fell, then dropping 280ft and climbing 261ft to Little Dun Fell, dropping a further 261ft before the 430ft drag up to the summit of Cross Fell, which at 2930ft is the highest point on the whole of the walk and which meant that I had climbed 2330ft since leaving Dufton 8½ MLS and 5 hours ago!

The incredible panorama far out-weighed the effort taken to reach the top. There, spread out before me was the breathtaking vista of the Lake District covered by a halo of thin cloud. With glorious blue skies above, it gave the mountain peaks a feeling of detachment from their earthly roots, as if there were two lands; one below where the mortals lived and toiled, and the one above where the Gods danced on veiled mountaintops.

Please let me build a house here, I'll promise I'll be quiet!

Cross Fell looking towards Cumbria

I sat for what seemed perpetuity, looking and wishing, but like all good things it had to come to an end for time waits for no man as someone once said and there were still 12½ MLS to go before this day's journey ended. Regrettably, I pushed on, thankful in the knowledge that from here on in it's all downhill (elevation wise that is). I stopped at the bothy just the other side of Cross Fell for lunch, taking the chance to refill my water bottle and remove my boots to let my feet breath. I say lunch, but it only consisted of a Marathon bar, biscuits and a cup of tea, but it was lunch to me. All the time I was sitting there I was constantly 'buzzed' by low flying jets; reminding me that civilisation was still out there. As if I needed reminding, I was going back to it in five days time?

Refreshed, I gathered my bits and my body and started off on what I thought was going to be an easy afternoon's walk down to Garrigill, and thence onto Alston. Not so. The next six miles were of endless, boring, uneven, rocky, potholed, brain numbing, ankle grinding trudge. The track seemed like it was going to go on forever! Every time I checked the map it said that just over the next rise the path would start to drop down to the village. But every time I reached the said rise there was another one, and then another one, and another! I reached the point where I felt like stopping where I was and setting up camp there and then, but I was miles away from provisions, sanctuary and pubs. So, with no alternative, I pushed myself on and ever on, eventually reaching Garrigill some two hours later. I found it amusing to find that this track used to be an old corpse road used for transporting the dead from Garrigill to burial grounds in the South Tyne Valley. I had the feeling that maybe some of them weren't properly dead until they made the journey along the track, and then they probably died of boredom?

There is also evidence of extensive mining in the area by the abundance of fluorspar; a mauve coloured crystal found lying here and there along the track. This is a by-product of mining and thought of as quite useless at one time but is now used as a flux in the making of steel.

Garrigill is another one of those pretty little northern villages, although not as pretty as Dufton, it still has its own charm. By pure coincidence, just as I was walking through the village, the three drinking companions from Tan Hill Inn emerged from the local tavern, obviously having partaken of the local spring water. We walked together for the rest of the day, chatting about this and that and nothing in particular. They did probably tell me their names but I'm buggered if I can remember them? I assumed that they must have left quite early this morning because nobody passed me on the path, but they assured me they didn't leave Dufton until 9 am? It wasn't until I thought about it that I remember hearing voices passing outside the bothy, which must have been them? "Christ!" I thought to myself. "How could they start out two hours after me and still arrive half hour before I did?" But then when I thought about it, they weren't carrying a 50lb rucksack and they were sleeping in comfortable warm beds every night with a cooked breakfast waiting for them in the morning; that made all the difference. While every day I had to rise at the crack of dawn and sit inside my cramped tent cooking eggs, bacon, sausage and tea over a single flame, then having to clean up, collapse my tent and pack that into my rucksack along with my sleeping bag, clothes, mess tins, gas stove, torch, maps, sleeping mat etc, they were being woken gently by some dusky Y.H.A. maiden around midmorning, led down to a food-laden table where they feasted to their hearts content and then, with pre-packed lunches, were given a hero's farewell and ushered on their way made easier by a rose petal carpet laid especially for their departure. But I wouldn't have swapped places for the world!

A couple of miles outside Alston the Way becomes confusing, so much so in fact that two of my companions thought it went one way and the other thought it went somewhere completely different. This left me in the middle not knowing which one to follow? Eventually, I plumped for the path that the pair had chosen as the other guy seemed a bit headstrong and probably was going in the wrong direction. As it was, by the time I made up my mind who to follow the others had disappeared and I was back on my own again? Things were now starting to get desperate as my water bottle was practically empty and the sun was beating down relentlessly. I had to find water soon as I was starting to feel decidedly unwell. This wasn't actually forthcoming until I reached the campsite and that was only after trudging from one end of the town to the other.

The site was marked quite clearly on the map but not anywhere else. I had actually walked past the site entrance, which was down the side of a petrol garage, while the owner, who was also the garage attendant, watched me walk past, obviously aware of the fact that I was looking for the said site.

I had gone about a mile out the other side of the town before I realised I had missed the camp. By now, due to dehydration and fatigue, I was beginning to feel demoralised and could have quite easily collapsed by the roadside and refused to move. I was totally sapped of energy and it took me all of my resolve and remaining strength to turn round and head back. As I neared the garage I noticed the camper from the tent next to mine at Dufton walk up to the attendant and ask him about the site and was duly pointed in the right direction. With hope renewed I quickened my pace and did the same, eventually collapsing in a heap on the grass.

The first thing I did once I managed to drag myself to my feet was head for the nearest standpipe where I drank long and deep. Some 20mins later, and with body renewed and energy returning, I set about the erection of my tent. This happened to be next to my camping companion Paul, a pleasant chap of about 40 years with a big bushy beard and the sort of demeanour that indicated years of backpacking under his belt. After showering I decided to venture into town in the hope of finding a supermarket open so as to stock up on food, but this proved fruitless. Instead, I ended up in the up-market café feasting on pizza and chips followed as usual with endless cups of tea.

My hunger pains abated, I retraced my steps to the campsite and relieved Paul of his guard duties while he went off in search of a pub that did bar meals. My body ached and fatigue was getting the better of me, so I decided to book myself in for an early night. But, because the evening was still youngish, I reasoned that an hour spent washing and drying my clothes would be an hour well spent and not really eat into my slumber time. Three hours and several naps later saw me emerge bleary-eyed from the laundry room due to an extremely slow and inefficient tumble dryer. It was dark, it was cold, and I was dead on my feet. I dragged myself to my little tent, slid myself into my cosy sleeping bag and didn't so much as drift off to sleep, more like I threw myself into the arms of Morpheus without so much as a by your leave.

Chapter 14
Alston to Greenhead

Day 11

Distance 17mls
Total 200mls

Although I didn't know it at the time, today was going to be one of the most boring days walking as regards scenery.

I awoke to the sounds and smells of breakfast being cooked in Paul's tent, leaving me with highly excited gastric juices before I had even emerged from my sleeping bag. I hurriedly dressed, looking forward to a gastronomic delight of oily eggs, fatty bacon, greasy sausages and campfire beans, (anybody who's seen Blazing Saddles will know what I'm on about). But then it suddenly hit me? I had forgotten about the shops being shut last night, which meant that I didn't have anything for breakfast this morning! Oh, how my guts complained! All the time I was packing up all I could hear was "So that's it then? I don't get anything today? I have to starve do I?" Of course, you have to be able to interpret stomach rumblings to understand what was being said, but that was the basic gist of it. Paul looked at me inquisitively as I passed him after packing my tent away, so I explained that I wasn't very hungry and that I would get some mileage under my belt before I stopped for brekkies. I don't think this convinced him for he offered to put some scraps in a 'doggie bag' for me, but I graciously declined and, adding another hole to my quickly receding belt, I strolled out of the campsite, casually glancing a hopeful eye at the waste bins just in case someone had discarded a half-eaten rump steak or pork chop from the previous night. I made directly for the local sell-it-all garage in the hope of purchasing anything that resembled a meal, but instead was confronted with an array of chocolate bars and crisps and, although they are both quite good energy sources in their own right, it wasn't what I had in mind as a wholesome and filling breakfast.

The path made its way back out of the village and crossed the River South Tyne before turning up a track to walk alongside the other bank. From here the river is followed for about a mile before eventually turning off and cutting across the A689 to carry on over some open fields where the Gilderdale Burn is met and crossed. A little further on the road is re-crossed, which seems a bit pointless as to follow the road is only about a mile in length, but by crossing the fields the distance is increased to a mile and a half with no added scenery to compensate for the extra yardage? For the next couple of miles, the way wove through countless gates and stiles before passing under an old viaduct of a railway which used to run between Alston and Haltwhistle, but which is now sadly disused except as a route for walkers. Here, a tributary of the South Tyne is met and leads you through a small flowery glade enclosed by trees which gives one the warm feeling of seclusion and security before the river proper is encountered, accompanying you all the way to the small hamlet of Slaggyford. Without detailed information, it's difficult to follow the route out of the village, which is my excuse for having to ask the way of a couple of locals who pointed me along the old railway telling me that I would meet the P.W. about half a mile further on where it passes under a small bridge. True to their word, I found the path and rejoined it.

Viaduct at Slaggyford

Everything was fairly simple from here on in as the path became part of the Maiden Way for the next 2½mls. This is an old Roman road that linked Kirkby Thorpe with the main fort at Carvoran at Hadrian's Wall. This is where things started to get boring as the surrounding countryside began to flatten out due to the end of the Pennines, or at least the end of the high Pennines, and, according to Wainwright, should signify the end of the Pennine Way itself. But fortunately for me and countless others, it doesn't. Once again the A689 is crossed as the way continues its boring journey, broken only by the welcome intrusion of Hartley Burn, which is akin to an oasis in the desert but being more for its aesthetic attributes than its life-saving values.

The tiny hamlet of Ulpham now comes into view some half a mile away and the pace quickened in the hope of finding refreshments. I was soaking in the peace and quiet of the open farmland when suddenly WHOOSH, BANG! A low flying jet screamed overhead, pursued by another, and another each time making me duck reflexively. It was an untimely and intrusive way to be reminded that somewhere in the world all was not well.

As I approached Ulpham I suddenly realised I was walking through a field full of bulls! Young, frisky bulls! Young, frisky bulls that probably wanted to show their mates how squishy a backpacker is. I dogged back and forth trying to avoid these male bovines like the plague but only managed instead to end up stepping in endless bullpats, (slightly larger and more macho than a cowpat). I finally made it to the farm gate unscathed only to find it guarded by a rather burly, determined-looking young bullock. I turned to find an alternative escape only to be confronted by the others now standing together as if to bar any form of retreat and realised they'd out-manoeuvred me in a pincer movement. It was now between me and Arnie!

Knowing they could smell fear (they didn't need to be downwind to smell mine!) I decided the best course of action was to be firm, even though my insides were shaking like an MP filling out a tax return. Staring him straight in the eyes I shouted, "SHOO!"

Nothing.

"BUGGER OFF OUT OF IT!!"

He didn't even blink.

I clapped my hands and waved my arms. He just stood there without flinching. 'What the hell am I going to do?' I thought to myself, wondering if at any moment he was going to charge at me knowing the only place to run would be straight into his mates who were waiting with hooves drawn. Just then, I accidentally dropped my map, and, as I bent down to retrieve it, he suddenly bolted and ran for the cover of the barn! Seizing the opportunity before any of Arnie's mates stepped in for a leadership takeover bid; I darted for the gate and escaped through to the farm track on the other side. At this point, Arnie started to wander back over like a schoolboy full of bravado, probably telling his mates "Yeah, well lucky for him he ran when he did cos I was just about to have him, wan I!"

With this fiasco over it was then a simple matter of an easy walk across the gentle slopes of Round Hill and Black Hill (fortunately not the same Black Hill of 170 miles previous), down and through the clay pit excavation works where you emerge onto the A69. Greenhead is now only a matter of a half mile away by road but to follow the P.W. would add to the journey and take me around the back of the village. So, instead, I turned down along the road and entered Greenhead by the front door. The first place I made for was the local garage cum general store and set about buying a damn good meal for this evening and a hearty breakfast for tomorrow. I then made my way about half a mile up the road to the campsite.

The site, the Roam and Rest Caravan Site, to give it it's full title, was the most pleasant, clean, neat and hygienic campsite I had ever been to and made camping a joy, especially after some of the sites I had stayed at along the way. It really was a site for sore feet! The toilet blocks were sparkling clean with pot plants and flowers adorning the walls and cubicles. There was a spotless stainless steel sink outside under cover for dishwashing that gave plenty of hot water. The grass looked like it had been cut with scissors and the gravel drive looked like it had been Hoovered! All in all, it made for a delightful and amiable stay, albeit for only one night.

Dinner consisted that evening of beef burgers and mashed potato, followed by tinned rice pudding and copious mugs of tea. Once fed I showered in luxury, put on my 'civvies' and headed for the nearest telephone box to report in, which just happened to be opposite the local pub, and of course, I had to partake of the local brews, it would be rude not to? On entering I found the Three Amigo's and Paul already sampling the waters, so I had no choice but to join them. There was also a jukebox in the pub playing quietly and on further investigation I found that it had my two favourite tracks on it, namely Led Zeppelin's 'Stairway to Heaven' (also my favourite band), and Fleetwood Mac's 'Albatross'. I sat there in total bliss, drinking real ale and listening to real music!

Tomorrow was going to be 22 miles of trudge, some of it over Hadrian's Wall, so, alas, only two pints later saw me making my way back to my tent. In doing so I found another camper had pitched up right next to me, even though there was plenty of space around the site? Oh well, that's his problem, I'm up at 5 in the morning, then he'll wish he'd camped somewhere else?

I'd also noticed a complete absence of Doris since leaving the Tan Hill Inn? Had she finally thrown in the towel? Had the weight she was carrying done for her going over Cross Fell? Had the dog finally had enough and buried her somewhere along the Corpse Road? I suppose I'll never know?

Chapter 15
Greenhead to Bellingham

Day 12

Distance 22mls
Total 215mls

My theory was proven correct. At precisely 5 a.m. I awoke to the sound of my watch alarm buzzing in my tin mug (it was the only way I could hear it), and by 5.15 I was cooking a breakfast of eggs, bacon and spaghetti, all the time listening to the moanings and stirrings of my next-tent neighbour. "Serves you right?" I thought, "That will teach you not to pitch so close when you've got the whole campsite to choose from!"

I was eventually packed up and gone by 6.30, loathing to leave such a beautiful campsite. But leave it I did picking up the P.W. a few hundred yards further on down the road. From here Thirlwall Castle (remains of), could be seen in all its morning glory, gazing ominously down from its hill as if still tempting upstarts to try to breach its fortifications.

Thirlwall castle, remains of

The path picks up a steep winding farm track just beneath the castle which soon leads out onto walled grasslands and where I had my first encounter with some long-haired cows, although I'll swear under oath they were bison in sheep's clothing? Worse still, they started following me and, having left my elephant gun back home, I decided to do the heroic thing and quicken my pace. Unfortunately, they did the same and by the time I had reached the stile at the other end of the field, I think I could have qualified for the SAS training run over the Brecon Beacons! Now, please don't take this to mean I'm frightened of animals, big animals, it's just that when you've got a consolidated weight of around 300 tons bearing down on you and all you've got between you and them is a couple of layers of fabric, a few aluminium pots and some synthetic sleeping bag filling, I think the saving of one human life far outweighs the love felt for big, furry animals?

I'd made up my mind this morning that the three musketeers were not going to outdo me today, knowing that they didn't usually leave the YHA until around 9.30 a.m. I was already three hours ahead of them, so I had a fighting chance, and also the weather was being kind to me, being warm and sunny but with a cool breeze blowing. Half a mile further on I reached Hadrian's Wall where some of the most amazing views could be seen looking east towards Newcastle-Upon-Tyne, and west towards Cumbria. The wall in places looked badly in need of repair and I wondered why some local brickies hadn't put in a quote for the work, considering the building industry was in such a bad state in this part of the country. Obviously, they need us southerners to point it out. I pushed on ignoring the condition of the wall and just stuck to admiring the beautiful scenery laid out like a feast below me, both on this side and the other.

Three miles later found me eating fruit cake and drinking tea at a van in a car park by a small pond, problem is that fruitcake is one of my weaknesses, so I treated myself to two chunks in the end and the tea washed it down a treat, not only that but my ever decreasing belt showed I had room for it now. Refuelled, I set off again for another bout of ups and downs. This turned out to be an exhausting part of the days walk for no sooner had I descended one hill, I had to climb another almost immediately, giving me no chance of rest in between. Just before 208 miles were reached I came upon Milecastle 39, apparently one of the many outposts along the wall. The problem was that although there was a total absence of Roman gladiators here now, it was made up for by hundreds of screaming school kids out baying for blood. If I had any thoughts about lingering here for peace, rest, scenery or historic interest, it was soon put paid to by this latter-day invasion of young barbarian's intent on scaring the life out of one more Sassenach! I soon showed them what I was made of and, deftly sidestepping ice-creams, pencils, tape measures, clipboards and a host of other weapons, I reached the other side of the 'castle' and quickly made my way up to the ridge of the hill, smug in the knowledge that I had single-handedly fought off a heavily outnumbered attack on my person.

Once Rapishaw Gap was met the route turned due north and headed towards a dense coniferous plantation known as Walk Forest South, Central and North, in that order. The path here became a lot easier as there was no climbing to do and no kids underfoot and, due to my love of forests, it became more enjoyable. It was while crossing some open land between Walk Forest South and Central that I came upon Paul and another fellow walker having lunch. "What time did you leave Greenhead?" I enquired and was told 6 am, which explained why they were sitting here eating and I wasn't. But instead of joining them I pushed on further, eventually finding myself a spot in the forest off the track where I took my boots off and had a brew-up, relaxing back in the grass and just looking up at the clear blue sky through the canopy of green overhead. I could have stayed there for ages but time pressed on, so half an hour later saw me up and back on the path heading into the North Forest. I eventually reached the edge of the tree line only to be met by the three Y.H.A's lying in the grass eating apples. I couldn't believe it! First Paul and his friend, and now these three!!!

"You're not telling me you left at 9.30 this morning?" I said, sounding rather flummoxed.

"No!" they replied, "It was about 8.30, we wanted an early start."

I couldn't believe what I was hearing? Even with a two-hour start they could still catch up and overtake me! But when? It must have been while I was having a cuppa in the forest? I walked away totally bewildered, leaving them still happily lazing in the grass.

I passed up the opportunity to have cream teas at Horneystead Farm, even though I was dying for one, and settled instead for another swig from my water bottle. By the time I reached Houxty Burn the said bottle was running low so I opted for a refill from the stream. But, just as I bent down, I dropped the Puritab into the water and, as the others were in my rucksack which I couldn't be bothered to take off, I decided to fill my bottle anyway, which was my first stupid mistake as I had no idea if the water was safe to drink?. With the sun blazing down my thirst increased by the minute and the water decreased by the mouthful, so I decided to call at a farm called Shitlington Hall and throw myself at their mercy. Problem was there was nobody in. Now I was in a dilemma. I was dehydrating quickly and in urgent need of water. It was then that I noticed the tap outside their backdoor and so took it upon myself to borrow some water from it, the intention being to send it back later once I'd finished with it! That's when I did the second stupid thing. Instead of drinking what was left from the bottle before refilling, I topped up on top of what was already there and, it wasn't until I came to drink it that I found it was vile tasting and had a cloudy colour, which meant I had to pour it all away! Now things were getting desperate. From what I could tell from the map there was no hope of getting any water until I reached Bellingham, another three miles away. But then luck! I came across a small brownish stream running across a farm track, but where it flowed over rocks it looked pretty clear. So I took a chance and filled my bottle. My third stupid mistake was to drink the water without purifying it first, but fortunately, luck was on my side and I had no after effects.

From here on in the last three miles were a drag, in so much as that because of the heat I was practically having to drag my feet every inch of the way. But once the B6320 was met it heralded the home stretch. Only another mile and a half of blazing sun and dehydration to go! Would I last? What made things worse was the crossing of the River North Tyne, a clear, fast-flowing and inviting deluge of drinkable water. Unfortunately, all of it flowing under a road bridge with no possible access down to its edge. All I could do was stand and drool. I dragged myself away and entered the town along the main high street, looking this way and that for any sign of a campsite or horse trough. I found neither, eventually having to ask at a local shop for directions. Even *they* didn't know where the site was, only what road it was on? As I emerged from the shop I bumped into Paul and his friend again and found that he was also looking for the same site, although his friend went off to another. Together we spent the next half hour trudging up and down the road looking for the damn thing! We even knocked at the local Police station only to find no one was in? Very disconcerting! And then by chance, we noticed a cottage across the road with the same name as the site we were looking for. We knocked and found that the site belonged to the owner and that it could be found behind the cowsheds across the road. With hearts in mouths we re-crossed the road, opened a small farm gate situated between two cottages and walked around the back of the sheds to find a large open field with one other tent already pitched. Thus relieved for the day to be over I dumped my rucksack and quickly found a standpipe where I drank long and deep, so deep, in fact, you could hear it squelching in my boots.

After pitching up, we both strolled up to the local 8-till-late shop and bought our bits and bobs for supper and breakfast. As a matter of fact, I decided to treat myself to a tin of peaches and a can of evaporated milk as a dessert. Problem was that when I opened it I found I'd bought a tin of condensed sweetened cream instead, which was absolutely sickening, so I had to settle for raw peaches instead. Such is life.

I had just started showering as Paul was drying himself off when he asked if I fancied going for a jar tonight. At first, I declined the offer as money was getting tight, but then on second thoughts said that I might just pop up for a pint later on. Truth was that I'd already made up my mind to go within the first two seconds of him asking me! Fifteen minutes later saw me walking in the direction of the Kings Head for refreshments and I'd just stopped to look in a shop window at some countryside books who should accost me? No, not Doris and her wonder dog, but the three companions, all looking totally refreshed as if they hadn't done anything more than enjoy a bus ride over from Greenhead! "Coming for a pint?" they asked, already knowing the answer, and as luck would have it they were going to the same pub, so we all bowled in together.

I was really looking forward to a pint of local real ale and could see three different types on the bar, the worst of these being Trophy bitter, so I opted for the first.

"Sorry," said the barmaid, "We've run out of that."

'Bugger!' I thought. "Never mind, I'll have a pint of the other," I said.

"Sorry," came the echoed reply, "That's fresh in today and hasn't settled yet."

Bloody bugger!

"We've got Trophy?" she offered like an eager salesman desperate to sell an unwanted product knowing that a sale was guaranteed.

So the rest of the evening was spent trying to enjoy my three pints of Trophy, listening to Paul's friend who just happened to be one of those walking encyclopaedias who knew everything there was to know about the Pennine Way. Like the fact that by the time you finish the walk you would have climbed the equivalent of over two and a half times the height of Everest; and that the quickest time it had been completed in was 2.75 days; and that the average man loses 'X' calories per mile, and so on and so on... As a matter of fact, I thought at the beginning of the walk I might become one of those statistics and be the first person ever to attempt the Pennine Way on crutches? Add to this the fact that he originally came from Bishops Stortford, a town only nine miles from me which meant he kept saying things like do you know such-and-such place and have you walked so-and-so yet? I couldn't wait to escape from him, and the beer. So around 9.30 I bade them all goodnight and departed for a sound night's sleep.

Tomorrow was only going to be a short one so I could afford a half hours lay-in in the morning. Oh, what bliss!

Chapter 16
Bellingham to Byrness

Day 13

Distance 16mls
Total 241mls

Thursday morning saw me up with the lark. It also saw me up with the cows as the field was slowly filling up with them. I didn't care today who left earliest, or who made it to Byrness first. I was happier in the fact that I'd made it as far as I had considering last year's dismal attempt. Unlike all the other mornings I can't remember what I had for breakfast, but it was probably something like eggs, bacon, sausages, and beans, all washed down with a mug or two of tea. Just guessing?

Paul wasn't leaving till later, so I pushed off around 7.30 making my way up a small 'B' road which passed the YHA where I stopped and wondered if I should do the decent thing and give my three friends an early morning call? But I decided to leave them sleep and dream for all was at peace with the world on this pleasant sunny morn. A few minutes later I was climbing the steep concrete track that leads up to Blakelow Farm, already sweating profusely but this time with plenty of water to combat thirst. The path leads through the centre of the farmyard and out on to open moorland where the scenery was pretty non-descript but promised to improve later.

Something I hadn't mentioned for the past few days was my leg, the reason being that, with the aid of an elasticated bandage, the muscle had sorted itself. The ankle was still troublesome, but bearable. So, as far as finishing the walk was concerned, everything was looking good.

The next four miles were nothing to write home about, so I didn't. As I approached the gentle slopes of Deer Play (1183ft) I turned to find I had a harem of sheep following me, obviously mistaking me for their provider, and no amount of 'shooing' or constructive argument on my part would convince them otherwise. So now I was stuck with around 40 sheep that looked intent on following me into Scotland where I would more than likely be arrested for rustling, which is still probably a hanging offence north of the border. I increased my pace in the hope of tiring them out but to no avail. In the end, I just settled for ignoring them in the hope that they'll go away, like any normal woman who's being ignored. After a couple of hundred yards, I lost my patience and decided that the only thing to do was to turn round quickly and shout loudly in the hope of frightening them off. So I took a deep breath, spun round on my heels and yelled "BUGGER OFF!" at the top of my voice, only to find that they had already buggered off some 50 yards before. They say in space, nobody can hear you scream. In open moorland, nobody can hear you scream obscenities at the sheep. The only compensation was that Paul and the other three all had this to come.

I pressed on exactly one mile to Lord's Shaw (1167ft) still not really impressed by the surrounding countryside, but then I'd been spoilt by such marvels as Pen-y-Ghent, Cross fell, Kinder Scout, Malham Cove, High Cup and many, many more, and, from what I had read, there were still plenty more to come. The sights and the climbing weren't over yet.

The path became quite indistinctive from here on so I ended up dragging myself through deep heather until the summit of Padon Hill (1240ft) was reached, this being the highest point attained since leaving Cross Fell. Once the top was met the path proper was regained and followed to Brownrigg Head (1911ft), which marked the descent down into Redesdale Forest, where the next six miles were to be spent among endless rows of conifers. After four miles the path arrives at a tiny hamlet with a not so tiny name of Blakehopeburnhaugh, which, when roughly translated means 'Blake in a sheltered valley on the flat land by a river', or words to that effect, and considering there was nothing really there, it didn't seem worthy of such a convoluted name.

Path into Redesdale Forest

From this point on the path turned down off the forest track to follow the River Rede until it emerged at the back of a church in Byrness, where the first thing I did was to make straight for the service station and café and satisfied my grumbling stomach.

With hunger pains abated I opted for a visit to the only shop for a replenishment of stocks. This meant walking from one end of the village to the other, but I had plenty of time so what the heck! I reached the YHA, which is situated in a small housing estate, only to find a complete absence of shop which should have been next door? On enquiring of some locals, I found that the shop had been closed down over a year ago and the only place to purchase anything now was yes, you guessed it, the garage shop at the other end of the village where I had just walked from! So back I trudged and re-entered the shop explaining to the girl behind the counter what I'd done.

"Well," she said, "If you had asked me I would have told you about the shop?"

"True," I replied, biting my tongue, "But if I thought there was any reason to ask you, I would have, but seeing as there wasn't, I didn't!"

This totally threw her and she fixed me with a cold, icy stare that even this far north I could translate as "Oh, fuck off!"

"Anyway," I carried on, "I'd like seven cartons of orange juice, a tin of beans and a tin of rice pudding, please."

I could see her trying to figure out why I would need seven cartons of juice, but I wasn't in the mood to enlighten her. The actual reason was that between Byrness and Kirk Yetholm, tomorrows destination, there wasn't any water, not even a farmhouse to call at unless you deviate quite a distance from the path, which if you did there would be no hope of finishing the walk in one day, which was my objective.

I left with a carrier bag full of goodies and the shop girl went back to playing with her friend's baby who was in the shop at the time, making stupid goo goo and gaa gaa noises, the girl that is not the baby. The child probably could have sat there and discussed the theory of relativity, or explained E=MC2, or even theorised on the possibility of an existential deity had they asked him, but why bother when the limit of intelligence of those conversing with him only went as far as making nonsensical goo goo and gaa gaa noises?

I made a decision at this point to push on another five miles or so instead of camping up in the village for the night. It was still only around 4 pm, so there was ample time and plenty of light, plus it would make things easier for tomorrow which, judging by the stories and the map, it needed to be. Half an hour later I was glad I'd made the choice to carry on for that's how long it took me to cover half a mile of ground, all of it in an extremely steep, upward direction to Byrness Hill. Around 700ft was climbed in that distance, the last 200 or so on all fours with rucksack on back and carrier bag in hand. But once the hill's summit had been reached I could sit back and recover while looking back over Redesdale Forest and south towards Padon Hill and Deer Play, sad that it was nearly all at an end.

Next stop was Windy Crag, aptly named because it was so bloody windy up there! Yet, as soon as I dropped a few feet off the top it became calm again. Strange? A mile later, Ravens Knowe was conquered and, at 1729ft, was the last big climb of today, the rest would be waiting for me tomorrow.

Bryness reservoir from Windy Crag

I walked down Ogre Hill keeping a wary eye open for marauding trolls and finally came upon the wire fence that designates the English/Scottish border. It was here that I decided to call it a day and camp for the night. I pitched quite close to the fence but obviously on the English side just so I didn't lose my rights as an Englishman if I became embroiled in a border skirmish. Well you can't take any chances, can you?

It was now around 6 pm and I was feeling peckish, so I opened the tin of rice pudding and opted for heating it up in the tin rather than use a dish for there was not enough water for cleaning. I sat there for ages heating and stirring, stirring and heating, and in the end, due to boredom, decided to eat it. It was still stone cold! The only bit that wasn't was right at the bottom, and that was burnt!! So, I sat there for the next 15 minutes trying to eat cold rice pudding. I finally managed it due to hunger and then promptly washed it down with cold orange juice. How I kept it all down I'll never know?

I sat there watching the sun set behind the trees and listened to the wildlife preparing for nightfall, either avoiding it or befriending it, and knew there wasn't another soul about up here to spoil my solitude and peace. Oh, what bliss!

By 9 pm I got my head down for to be sure of covering the 20 or so miles to Kirk Yetholm tomorrow I needed to be up around 4 am, so I could do with all the sleep I can get.

Chapter 17
Border fence to Kirk Yetholm

Day 14

Distance 25mls
Total 270 mls

I woke up cold but eager with a still darkness around me amplifying the smallest of sounds. It was 4 am and dawn's early light was on the verge of unveiling itself to the world for the trillionth time since the creation of the earth. As regards time, I didn't exist, and I was glad I didn't because it was bloody cold! On emerging from my tent I found it to be covered in ice with a thick frost on the grass, making the small valley where I was camped look like being on an ice floe, albeit a green ice floe.

As I stood there, a pinprick shaft of orange/red light broke through above the lip of the Cheviots and silhouetted the hills drastically against the cloudless morning sky. It brought a lump to my throat to be up here in all this natural beauty. Just me, the wildlife and Mother Nature at her most endearing. The only thing that spoilt the scene was the MoD notice that warned the walker that he was on the edge of a large firing range and should keep to the path if he wanted to arrive at his destination with all his limbs still intact and not looking like a colander, although not in so many words.

Sunrise over the Cheviots

I decided to breakfast, which consisted this morning of cold baked beans due to the same problem that befell my rice pudding last night which, true to form, was washed down with cold orange juice. Yuck! But it's surprising what your stomach can take when it has to.

As I stood watching the day unfolding a sudden realisation washed over me.

"Well, Dave," I said to myself. "This is it, the last day! This is what you first started planning for 14 years ago and never thought you'd achieve, never thought you'd realise your dream. But here it is, the last day; then it's all over." Then I thought to myself 'Is it the last day? Will it all be over by this afternoon? What could befall me all alone up here in the wilderness?' Then I thought, 'Bugger it! Who knows, so let's get on with it and find out?'

I dismantled my tent for the last time, shook the ice from it, stuffed everything neatly into my rucksack, tightened my boot laces, picked up my carrier bag and made sure there was no trace of my night's camp before climbing the stile over the border fence into Scotland. "Hoots mon, ah didne feel onie different laddie!" Sorry, it must have been something they put in the Scots air?

I cut along by the fence before skirting the mounds of earth that signify some old Roman camps and climbed the gentle slopes of Greystone Brae and then onto Lamb Hill some five miles distant, all the time keeping on roughly the same contour height. Just before Lamb Hill I passed a mountain refuge hut erected in cases of emergency while out on this desolate stretch of hillside and decided to look inside. I was amazed at how dry and comfy it was and what sort of consolation it would bring to any walker trapped out overnight. So much so in fact that I wished I stayed in it myself last night? I pushed ever onward and upward towards Beefstand Hill, which at 1842ft was only about 400ft higher than I was back at camp seven miles gone. The time now was getting on for around 7 am, and gazing north a sleepy looking Northumbria was just starting to go about its daily business, although most of the farmers had been doing that since around daybreak.

Early morning Cheviots

After the slightly smaller hill of Mozie Law had been visited there was a long, steep, boggy climb up to the 2034ft height of Windy Gyle. The way was so boggy in fact that I had to stop every 100ft or so to rest and remove the 40lb of peat stuck to my boots, each time making me feel like Apollo with his winged shoes until the next collection of peat had to be removed. I eventually made it and promptly sat down to admire the rolling hills all around me, some already conquered and some yet to be, while all the time the big one, the Cheviot, all 2676ft of it, the last major mountain to be climbed, stood there taunting me as if saying "You've still got me to go yet, pal?"

With the sun now beating down warm and comforting I had to force myself to stand and carry on. It was so peaceful and relaxing here I just wanted to lie down and go to sleep. But carry on I did, down to Road Butts some 300ft lower and a mile and a half away, then along to Kings Seat and a mile further on, after wading through more bogs, I began the steep ascent of Cairn Hill. On reaching the summit a decision must be made as to whether to deviate from the path and make the long trek to the top of the Cheviot, which is not actually part of the Pennine Way, or turn N.W. and head for civilisation? From what I understand, I did what most true devotees of the P.W. do, I turned N.W. and said: "Bugger the Cheviot, its 2½ miles there and back, all of it peat bog and there's sod all to see when you get there!"

From Cairn Hill to Auchope Cairn somebody had done the decent thing and laid some of the 'duck boards' last seen in Wuthering Heights country, but more to help stop the erosion of the mountain rather than help the walker, and they proved a blessing if the bogs underneath were anything to go by, not to mention the time saved.

Now, if these could just be extended back as far as Edale?

Auchope Cairn was to be the last major climb of the Way, being 2382ft high, but it was the descent that proved to be the toughest part of the mountain, it was practically vertical with loose rocks and scree, but it got you down fast! After descending some 700ft I came across another refuge hut where I decided to stop for a drink. Inside was bits of old candles and matches and a message telling you that if you want some water then you could make the steep descent to Hen Hole which, from where I was standing, looked pretty dodgy? Glad that I had the foresight to bring my own I drank up and readied myself for the last climb of the walk; the Schill; only 1985ft high and looking a doddle from the top of Auchope Cairn.

What looked a doddle from up there was now looking a killer from down here? Somebody must have a sick sense of humour? After all, that climbing done during the day with the last one being at the foot of the Cheviot you think it's all over and the walk into Kirk Yetholm will be heaven from that point onward. Then someone with a warped mind decides to throw in one last peak to test your resolve; one final challenge to divide the men from the boys; one last Everest. It was lucky I still kept my old school shorts! Once the top was reached I collapsed both from exhaustion and from relief and just sat there for ages, gazing at what was to be the last five miles of walking for this old body and wondering if I could make it? But, after serious thought, I decided I couldn't go on any further, so I turned round and headed back to Edale (some old backpackers humour there!)

The Schill looking NE

I looked back on what I had accomplished for that day and wasn't surprised I was totally knackered and ready to give up. It was then that I heard a voice and a shudder went through me. "Please don't say it's them?" I said to myself. "I couldn't take it. If they've caught up with me already then I might as well throw myself off the top!" I was just about to stand when a big shaggy dog appeared round the rock I was leaning against, followed by his master. I nearly cried with relief and decided there and then not to tempt fate any longer.

I know this wasn't a race and the only person I was in completion with was myself, but for once in my life, I wanted to experience the elation of coming first at something – and this was going to be it!

I dragged myself to my feet, tightened my straps, adjusted my belt and headed off down to the hill known as Black Hag where the path splits in two, one course heading down the valley to the road, and the other taking a high-level route over who knows where? I certainly didn't because I opted for the lower, easier one. The good news was that the path kept going in a downward direction, which was much favoured to the upward until the road was reached, whereupon it started going steeply up again? Drat!! I'm sure the road was put there as a last ditched effort to make me give up, but I didn't. I went for it and at exactly 3 pm on Friday 25th May 1990, I finished, nay, conquered the Pennine Way!

Yes, it was ended, completed, beaten, subjugated, assailed, overcome, defeated, trounced, concluded, terminated! Any adjective you choose to use. It was done, and so was I.

I entered a beautiful setting of a village green surrounded by cottages, all totally unspoilt as yet by tourism and, just as Wainwright had said, there were no brass bands to greet you, or young maidens ready to festoon you with floral wreaths or even an official of the town just to shake your hand and say "Well done, lad!" It had to be a silent, personal appreciation. One that left you empty because it was over. 14 years of planning and wishing on my part were now all gone. It was finished. OK so I'll have the photos and I'll write about this later, but it was over and only memories are left. But what memories!

With lump in throat I made my way to the Border Inn Hotel, the official finishing point of the walk, to sign the book and claim the free half pint bequeathed to all Pennine Way'ers by old Wainwright himself as a token of his admiration. I proudly marched up to the door, deposited my rucksack outside and tried the handle. Would you believe it, the bloody thing was shut!!! I peered through the windows in the hope it was a trick being played by the hotel staff on all who seek the rewarding half-pint. A wee Scottish jape where, as you stood there rattling the handle feeling unappreciated and unloved, they would suddenly fling open the doors and throw their arms around you, then hoist you up onto their shoulders and carry you victorious around the inn to the rapturous applause of all its patrons, but not a soul could be seen, anywhere. It was shut! I slumped down onto the bench seat outside, opened my carrier bag and consoled myself with my last remaining carton of orange juice. Well met the victorious hero? More like 'Turn the lights out when you're finished, mate!' Alas, more was to follow.

Crushed, I made for the bus stop so as to start the long, solitary journey home, only to find I'd missed the last bus! So I found a call box and rang home to give my wife the proud, exciting news. This was met with total indifference due to the fact that she wasn't happy with me doing it in the first place, saying that it would probably plunge us into debt. Unbeknown to both of us at the time, her concerns were to be highly prophetic, as I explained earlier.

The only bit of good news was that I had actually beaten the others. On the day it truly mattered to me, I'd done it; I'd actually come first for once. The boy from Essex who'd left school without a qualification to his name and hadn't really achieved much up to this point could now stand proud that, against all odds, had accomplished something others mocked him over. Boy, it felt good!!

I made my way to the youth hostel, which like the Inn, was also shut! (They must have known I was coming?) and sat down outside to await the arrival of the warden. While doing so, an elderly lady with a young child in tow walked up from a row of cottages and, noticing me looking obviously shattered and hot, enquired if I would care for a glass of orange. I couldn't believe it? She didn't know me from Adam, had never seen me before in her life, and here she was offering me refreshments? Had this been back home, you could be lying in the middle of the road, dying of dehydration and people wouldn't even spit on you. I readily accepted her offer and was told to just sit there and take it easy, which I did happily. About ten minutes later she returned with not only a tall glass of orange juice but also a full glass of milk and ice cubes to accompany both drinks! Now, this was hospitality! I thanked her gratefully and she left me with the glasses just telling me to hand them to the warden when I was done. Now, this was trust!

About two hours later the warden did appear but couldn't let me in due to the fact that they weren't ready, so I had to sit there for another half hour. Eventually, he did let me in and I immediately made for the showers where I spent a good 20 minutes under the soothing hot spray. I paid for the night's stay plus a cooked breakfast for the morning, the first one in 14 days that I wouldn't have to cook myself! Unfortunately, this left me with no cash, so I enquired of the warden whether they were likely to cash a cheque for me at the hotel.

"Oh yes, no problem," he said "But that probably won't be until they open the restaurant?"

"Ah!" I replied, "It's just I was going to go up for a couple of pints before I ate?"

"That's no problem?" said the warden, "Here, borrow a fiver, you can pay me back once you've got your cheque cashed."

I couldn't believe the trust and friendliness up here. Boy, had I led a sheltered life!

I sauntered up into the village and entered the Border Inn only to find the Three Amigos and Paul on their way out, having been in there for the last hour celebrating their success.

"Hello!" they said, "just got in?"

I felt huge delight in telling them that I'd actually arrived at 3 pm only to find the pub shut and had been down at the hostel ever since.

The feeling of achievement and proudness emanating from the five of us was so strong you could have bottled it and sold it to other budding Pennine Wayers to give them the courage to keep going when faced with adversity. Pats on the back completed, we all shook hands and congratulated each other on a walk well done. They then strode off down to the hostel and I entered the pub for my complimentary half pint as donated by A.W. himself to all those that complete the walk. I strode up to the bar, ordered my drink with a smug but satisfied grin on my face, and then realised that I had forgotten to bring with me his Pennine Way Companion book, which is a prerequisite for the free drink! Never mind, I took my drink, sat myself down and silently toasted A.W., and myself.

Once the restaurant was open I pigged out on steak and kidney pie and chips with mushy peas followed by chocolate cake and ice cream with coffee to end. Just as I finished the other lads returned and we sat for the rest of the evening drinking and joking and recalling all the good and bad bits, of which there were plenty to recall? It came out in conversation with Paul that a couple of years previously he'd taken five weeks off work and walked the 520 miles of the South-West Peninsular Coast Path which, some of you may be thinking, must make it the longest path in Britain and not the Pennine Way? Not so, because the Coast walk is a series of shorter paths which can be joined together to walk as one; whereas the PW is one continuous non-stop walk in its own right.

By the end of the evening we were all pretty well worse the wear for drink but happy in our achievements. And so with well-dones' exchanged and pats on the back exhausted, Paul and his mate staggered off to their campsite and the three companions and I weaved our weary but merry way back to the hostel. After 14 days under canvas, sleeping in a proper bed was an uneasy feeling and took some getting used to again, but I finally did and spent a peaceful nights slumber without having to worry about getting up early for another days walking. But my troubles weren't over yet. There was still the problem of getting back home to be dealt with and that was another venture in its own, which I'll tell you about tomorrow. But for now, night-night.

Author (second left) and companions outside Kirk Yetholm YMCA

Chapter 18
Return the Conquering Hero?

Day 14

Distance @ 450 miles

This should have been the easiest day of the whole venture. Just catch a bus to Kelso, change for Jedburgh, then down to Sheffield by rail to catch the return train to St Pancras, followed by a short trip on the underground to Liverpool St, with a final journey home to Harlow where I'd be picked up by my loving wife and kids. That is how it should have been – but it wasn't. What actually happened was a complete nightmare.

Saturday morning started just how Friday's ended, hot & sunny. By 8 am all four of us were up and sitting at the breakfast table awaiting a hearty meal of yes, you guessed it, eggs, bacon, sausage, tomatoes, fried bread etc, etc.... It was while eating this that I started to ask the warden the best way to get out of the village and head down to Sheffield. He promptly sought out his bus timetables and came up with the bad news that the bus from Kirk Yetholm actually gets into Kelso five minutes after the bus to Jedburgh leaves? This meant a four-hour wait until the next one and Jedburgh was the only place where you had a chance of getting to a major town. So now I was buggered, to say the least! How the hell was I going to get back to Sheffield from here? Fortunately enough my companions came up with an idea, saying that a friend of theirs was picking them up and if I talk to him nicely he might be able to help me out.

The friend finally turned up in a large Volvo estate so there was no problem about room, but could he help me? "Yes," he said after the others had spoken to him. "I'll drop you off in Newcastle if you wish; I've got to go past that way?" "Brilliant!" I said, "Problem solved!" We loaded up the car, said our goodbyes and thanks to the warden, jumped in and were away.

Leaving Kirk Yetholm was sad, even after just one night I felt I was part of the village already, having read about it hundreds of times and gazed at countless pictures, and now I had actually visited it, albeit briefly. More so I felt that with the Pennine Way I was leaving a friend, one I'd spent 14 days with and got to know intimately. I'd walked its hills, climbed its mountains, hated its bogs, loved its rivers, appreciated its wildlife and admired its grandeur. I can't say I knew the PW like the back of my hand, but I know it better than parts of Harlow, and I've lived there practically all my life.

The journey out of the village was a quiet one with each of us in our own way reminiscing silently the parts that we will remember forever.

Terry, the driver, finally broke the silence by asking where I came from, what I did etc. Then occurred one of those spooky instances of just how small a world we live in for at the time I was sub-contracting off a firm from Nottingham, which is where Terry came from. But even stranger still, he happened to be friends with the managing director of the said company! Unfortunately, work was something I didn't want to be reminded of just yet, that unpleasant experience was waiting for me when I returned.

It was an enjoyable journey in the warm sunshine, passing back through scenery like that experienced on the walk, but on a smaller and faster scale.

Eventually, we reached Newcastle, and a few minutes later the railway station. I collected my belongings from the back of the car, shook hands with the lads, wished them all well and hoped I'd see them on the Way again one day, thanked Terry for the lift and headed for the ticket office. As I approached the information desk I noticed on the overhead consoles that there was a train leaving soon for Kings Cross station, which was next to St Pancras and would save me messing about with trains from Sheffield. So I asked at the desk if it would be possible to transfer the ticket over for the other train and was told it couldn't be done unless I caught a train to Sheffield and then changed to the original one. So I agreed to this and asked how much extra it would cost me.

"Hold on," said the man at the desk, "I'll just check?"

I nearly fell through the floor!

"£37?" I said disbelievingly, "Just to get from here to Sheffield? But it only cost me £25 originally and that was for a return to Harlow??"

"Yes," he said, "But that's on a white saver ticket, today's a blue saver day, so it'll cost you extra even if you walk down to Sheffield!"

What the hell was I gonna do now? I had about £10 in my pocket and I was reluctant to use my chequebook too, especially for that much, so in the end, I opted for trying to find out how much it was by National Express coach to London. This meant taking the Metro to St James Park where I would find the coach station.

It was around 12noon when I joined the queue for the ticket information desk and it took me another 15 minutes before I got served.

"Can I help you?" the lady behind the desk enquired.

"Yes please, how much is it for a ticket to London?"

"£17.50." was the reply.

"Right!" I said, "I'll take one!"

"When do you want to leave?" was the next question.

"As soon as possible!" was my desperate reply.

"Well, there's a coach leaving at 12.30."

"Magic!" I said, "I'll take it."

"Oh, hold on?" came the reply, "That one's full, and the next one isn't till 3 pm."

"Damn it!" I exclaimed, "Well, it will have to be that one then?"

"You could have a word with the bus driver when he comes in?" she offered as some sought of solace, "He might be able to fit you in if somebody else has cancelled?"

"OK, thanks," I said miserably and sauntered off to have a cup of tea in the terminus cafe.

Terminal café was more like it? If you were waiting for a bus to take you somewhere to end it all then the café was sure to help you on your way. No windows. No air. No colour. Just four bare walls and hard, cold plastic seats. I just hoped there was a spare seat on the coach; I couldn't stand the thought of another 2½ hours stuck in here!

12.30 came and went and so did the coach, totally full up, not even a space on the luggage racks was available, so I resolved myself to having to go back and sit in the suicide suite of the Café Terminal. After just 15mins of this, I decided I couldn't take anymore and handed in my rucksack at the left luggage window and headed down to see what delights Newcastle town centre had to offer. I was dying for a pint but knew better than to walk into a Geordie pub with a southern accent, so I steered clear and settled for a can of coke instead. The shopping precinct was nothing to write home about, but at least it was clean and full of….shops.

After an hour of walking around and getting thoroughly bored, I headed back to the bus station for the last hour and hopefully a quick nap. The last hour I got; the quick nap I didn't. This was due to hoards of screaming little bastards, punching and kicking the shite out of each other, or children just expressing themselves, as they're called nowadays. So I sat there, reading and re-reading my newspaper until I knew every story off by heart, where the paper was printed and what typeset they used. Then finally it was here, the golden chariot that would whisk me away from all this and back to…all that. I took my place in line with all the other urban immigrants and one by one we boarded the London bound double-decker. I made straight for upstairs and did my usual trick of putting my rucksack on the seat next to me as a warning to others that I wanted to be left alone. It worked. I spent the next 5½ hours reading, eating, drinking and sleeping, mainly sleeping, without once being disturbed.

The bus finally pulled in to Victoria coach station at around 9 pm and I couldn't wait to get off and find the tube, knowing that at this rate I'd be lucky to get home before midnight. Five minutes later I was on a train heading for Liverpool St station when it suddenly occurred to me that if what the guy at Newcastle said was true then I would probably get stopped at the station and charged extra for my ticket? But as luck would have it there was no guard at the gate, so I just sailed through. I got up onto the platform just as a train was pulling out and enquired of the guard which was the train to Harlow?

"That one just leaving mate," he said with a wry smile. "If you run you may still be able to get on!"

The next 30 seconds saw me sprinting down the platform complete with a 50lb rucksack on my back in a record time that Ben Johnson would have been proud of!

I just made it before I ran out of concourse only to be greeted by the news that the trains were being terminated at Tottenham Hale due to track work. Instead, a bus was organised to pick us up and take us on a North London tour before depositing us at Cheshunt, where we could pick up the train again and hopefully carry on to Harlow. I couldn't believe what I was hearing? After 14 days and 270 miles of overcoming a sprained ankle, pulled muscles, blisters and some of the most gruelling countryside in the land, Big Brother was slowly beating me into submission. Little by little, over the course of the day he had worn me down. I was near ready to surrender and promised never to go wandering off enjoying myself again.

Tottenham Hale arrived and we all alighted, making our way to the buses waiting outside the station. I boarded the one at the rear knowing that it would be the most empty, but unfortunately was stuck with an idiot trying to impress three Japanese teenage girls with his exploits of world travel which, judging by the way he was describing things, sounded as if he had never got further than the Isle of Wight? Finally, the bus pulled up outside Cheshunt station and we all ran for the train hoping that it wouldn't leave before we got to it. We needn't have worried, it took a further 15 mins before it departed. I watched eagerly as the intermediate stations passed. First Broxbourne then Roydon and finally the one I had been waiting for since leaving Kirk Yetholm; Harlow!

I stepped off the train at 11.15 having spent over 13 hours travelling and looked at the familiar surroundings where 17 days earlier I had set out not knowing what to expect or whether it would be another failure. But here I was returned, triumphant! Then that worrying thought again. What if they stop me at the gate and demand extra money? This time I'd made up my mind that if it was an argument they wanted then I'd give them one, for it was here that I'd bought the ticket and explained to the guy when I was coming back, so it was his fault I had the wrong one! I pulled back my shoulders, puffed out my chest and with ticket in hand, I marched assuredly and steadfastly down the steps towards the gate, only to find yet again that there was no guard! Phew!!

It was just a case now of ringing home and getting my wife to come and pick me up. I couldn't believe it, no bloody answer! I had to resort to hailing a cab in the hope that there was enough money at home to pay for it. Once I finally did arrive home my wife, Sandy, who had been at my son, Kris's, football prize giving do when I rang, was there to greet me and also show me a banner that my daughter, Jamie, had strung up across the garage door saying "WELCOME HOME DAD". For me, that said it all.

I had set out on this journey to find out, amongst other things, if there was anything humorous about the Pennine Way. Well, I can safely say that, mixed in with the endless trudge through peat bogs, the agony of sheer unrelenting mountains, the drudgery of never-ending desolate moorlands, and the aches and pains of dragging myself and half a camping shop all over northern England, there were, as far as I could remember, some funny moments along the way, but at the time they weren't that evident.

Please do not take this book as being informative by any stretch; it's just one man's account of something which is attempted by scores of people every year, and not always successfully, as per my first attempt bears witness. But it may give a little insight, if not inspiration, for other amateurs like myself to get off your bums and try it. If it does, then the blood sweat and tears that went into writing this book, let alone walking the Pennine Way, has all been worthwhile. And who knows, I might do it again one day.....once I've stopped having treatment!

Border Inn, Kirk Yetholm

The End.